To Larry!
♡ Tricia 6-30-14

Leadership Lessons From History

A Study Guide Written for Physicians
& Other Healthcare Leaders

Calvin J. Maestro Jr., M.D., MBA/HCM

authorHOUSE®

AuthorHouse™
1663 Liberty Drive
Bloomington, IN 47403
www.authorhouse.com
Phone: 1 (800) 839-8640

© 2015 Calvin J. Maestro Jr., M.D., MBA/HCM. All rights reserved.

No part of this book may be reproduced, stored in a retrieval system, or transmitted by any means without the written permission of the author.

Published by AuthorHouse 01/19/2016

ISBN: 978-1-5049-0695-1 (sc)
ISBN: 978-1-5049-0696-8 (e)

Library of Congress Control Number: 2015906015

Print information available on the last page.

Any people depicted in stock imagery provided by Thinkstock are models, and such images are being used for illustrative purposes only.
Certain stock imagery © Thinkstock.

This book is printed on acid-free paper.

Because of the dynamic nature of the Internet, any web addresses or links contained in this book may have changed since publication and may no longer be valid. The views expressed in this work are solely those of the author and do not necessarily reflect the views of the publisher, and the publisher hereby disclaims any responsibility for them.

Summary

This is a book that you can read in one sitting. This also is a book that you will not soon forget. One part history lesson and one part storytelling, it combines humor and personal experiences to reveal how even the best of leaders and managers can flub up – or excel! Don't you make the same mistakes. Although intended for physicians new to leadership roles in this age of team-oriented healthcare management, anyone can benefit from its examples. Presented in no specific order, and often ranging far away from strict medical subjects, the reader can take his or her time to absorb the presented subject matters, be it military or administrative in nature. Additionally, there are a few stories about being a husband and father. Just don't forget to have fun reading them.

Dedication

This book is dedicated to my wife, Wendy, and my two children, David and Catherine.

Acknowledgements

I would like to thank all those throughout the years who, directly and indirectly, have helped me with this project. This includes the American College of Physician Executives (now called, American Association for Physician Leadership) who allowed me to give a poster presentation on the same subject, and the Michigan State Medical Society for running two of my examples in their publications. I also would like to thank my associates at work, the Alcona Health Center, and especially my good friend Dr. Andy Perez, one of the most talented individuals I've ever met. Lastly, I would like to thank the publisher for helping with the development and publication of this book.

Biography

Calvin J. Maestro, Jr., M.D., FAAFP, MBA/HCM

Dr. Maestro is a **board-certified family physician** currently practicing in a federally supported community rural health center in upper Michigan. He has had over 26 years of direct patient care experience and also 14 years' experience with administrative medicine, working for a number of healthcare insurers. He graduated from Fairleigh Dickinson University with a **B.S. Degree in Biology** and attended the **Newark Medical School at the University of Medicine & Dentistry in New Jersey** where he was the chief editor of his graduating class' yearbook. He received his **MBA in Healthcare Management from the University of Phoenix.** He has taught several courses for the University of Phoenix's Colleges of Nursing and Medical Management in Michigan. He has been an honorary **clinical assistant professor of medicine.** His fascination with EHRs extends back to 1989 when he computerized his own medical office.

Introduction

This was a labor of love in that I never started out to purposely write a book. I simply like to share my thoughts, knowledge, and experiences with others and my unique sense of humor often allows me to see the irony of it all, especially when it comes to the history of medicine. As chief editor of our medical school yearbook, I contacted a dozen medical Nobel Prize winners and asked them to write a message to our graduating class. I still have those letters. I also love to teach. When I taught undergraduate and graduate courses at a College of Nursing and also of Healthcare Management, I tried to bring the textbook and assigned readings to life. I challenged my students to think for themselves. I made them laugh. Often, I'd share the "dirty" background information that the readings cleaned up or left out. I knew that I had connected with my students when one of them interrupted me in the middle of a class presentation and called out, "Dr. Maestro, please stop. You're scaring us!" I now would like to share what I know with my fellow physicians and healthcare workers.

To some of you who are not accustomed to straight talk, what I have to say in this book may come across as a pleasant and humorous surprise – a breath of fresh air. Indeed, there are times when the emperor has no clothes! However, my critics may accuse me of being cynical and biased against non-medical leaders and administrators. In reply, let me say this: when I first started out as a medical director, I started a scrapbook; I'd cut out any of the applicable Dilbert cartoons, by Scott Adams, cartoon subjects that I had experienced at work, either directly or indirectly. After a few months, I stopped. I was cutting them all out!

The comments and examples in this book also are directed at my own profession. In my first freshman month of medical school classes, the Psychiatry Department professors taught us that, according to the latest studies, people were left-handed because they had suffered brain injury in the mothers' wombs. I then looked around the room and noticed that one-third of my medical school class was left-handed, including myself. Later on, the same professors quoted another study on left-handedness. As researchers tracked the proportion of the population that was left-handed, they noticed a significant drop-off in the older ages; there were hardly any left-handed people seventy-years or older left alive. They concluded that left-handed people died earlier as a result of accidents caused by living in a world that was predominantly right-handed. As it turned out, their finding was correct. However, the researchers of the study committed the common mistake of basing their conclusions on current and not past social norms and customs. Obviously, they never encountered my first grade teacher, a nun, at St. Augustine's Elementary School in Union City, New Jersey. She beat my left hand to death with a ruler while trying to switch me to writing with my right hand!

Lastly, I am in the intellectual debt of Alfred Jay Bollet, M.D., previously from the Yale University School of Medicine. We share a common fascination with medical history and his two books, *Plagues & Poxes* (Demos Medical Publications, 1987 & 2004), were instrumental in inspiring this one. Just recently, I became aware of the scholastic writings of H. William Dettmer. My examples would make a complementary bookend to his publication, *Strategic Navigation* (ASO Quality Press, 2003).

For further information on this book, or to contact the author, please access my personal web page at: www.maestrojr.us. You may also contact me on Facebook© or LinkedIn©.

Contents

Summary v
Dedication vii
Acknowledgements ix
Biography xi
Introduction xiii
Part 1   Title: "She Outranks Me" 1
Part 2   Title: "That Sinking Feeling" 3
Part 3-A Title: "Healthcare Stakeholders Also are Patients" 5
Part 3-B Title: "Five Stages of a Product Recall" 7
Part 3-C Title: "Denial: The First Stage of a Product Recall" 9
Part 3-D Title: "The Other Stages of Grief" 11
Part 3-E, Statements. Title: "Applying Elizabeth Kubler-Ross' Stages" 13
Part 4   Title: "Alexander's Greatness" 17
Part 5   Title: "High Flying Performance Incentives" 19
Part 6   Title: "Knowledge vs. Understanding" 23
Part 7   Title: "Marching Orders" 25
Part 8   Title: "The Game of Golf" 29
Part 9   Title: "The Truth About Healthcare Reform" 33
Part 10   Title: "Teaching Common Sense" 35
Part 11   Title: "Trust but Verify" 39
Part 12   Title: "Remember the Alamo" 41
Part 13   Title: "The Difference Between Accountability
               and Responsibility" 45
Part 14   Title: "True Visionary Leadership" 47
Part 15   Title: "Leadership Success vs. Ethics" 51
Part 16   Title: "Trust & the Horror of Infectious Diseases" 53
Part 17   Title: "Of Silos and System's Operational Performance" 57
Part 18   Title: "The Great Mouse Hunt" 59
Part 19   Title: "On EHR Form, Function & Purpose. Or,
               Still Waiting for Godot" 63

Part 20	Title: "Herd Mentality & Group Think"	65
Part 21	Title: "The Value of Stable Teamwork"	67
Part 22	Title: "Outcomes are Related to Process as Effectiveness is to Efficiency"	69
Part 23	Title: "Garbled Transmission"	73
Part 24	Title: "Adopting Business Ethics"	75
Part 25	Title: "Dead Horses"	79
Part 26	Title: "Leadership & Motivation"	81
Part 27	Title: "Sources of Inspiration"	85
Part 28	Title: "Loss of Vision"	87
Part 29	Title: "Life is About Pacing Yourself; Don't Run it as a Series of 100-Yard Dashes!"	89
Part 30	Title: "Promoting Effective People"	91
Part 31	Title: "Updates & the HMS Hood, and the Sinking of the Bismarck"	93
Part 32	Title: "Saying No!"	95
Part 33	Title: "Administrative Think!"	97
Part 34	Title: "The Need for a Devil's Advocate"	99
Part 35	Title: "Being a Leader Means Being Prepared"	103
Part 36	Title: "Whistle-Blowing"	105
Part 37	Title: "I like bats much better than bureaucrats"	109
Part 38	Title: "Making Operational Music Together"	113
Part 39	Title: "High Flying Performers"	117
Part 40	Title: "Supply Lines"	119
Part 41	Title: "Future Anticipation"	121
Part 42	Title: "Medical Providers are Being Stress Fractured"	123
Part 43	Title: "Leaders Need Champions"	127
Part 44	Title: "Keeping to One's Mission"	129
Part 45	Title: "Expert Advice"	131
Part 46	Title: 'Innovation'	135
Part 47	Title: "Procession"	137
Part 48	Title: "Cutbacks"	139
Part 49	Title: "The Value of Serendipity"	141
Part 50	Title: "The Value of Non-Events"	143
Part 51	Title: "The Captain of the Ship"	145
Part 52	Title: "Middle Managers"	147

Part 53 Title: "Magic Acts" 151
Part 54 Title: "Risk-Taking Leaders" 155
Part 55 Title: "Strategic Thinking" 159
Part 56 Title: "True Pay-for-Performance" 163

Leadership Lessons From History
Part 1

Title: "She Outranks Me"

During the American Civil War, the Union Army officers in charge of a particular military field hospital wanted a troublesome volunteer nurse removed from camp. In her zeal and enthusiasm to take care of the wounded soldiers, this female front-line healthcare worker routinely ignored standard military protocols. At times, she even was openly insubordinate to her superiors whenever they were not sufficiently supportive of her charges' care. Eventually, the officers appealed to their commander, General Sherman (of burning down Atlanta fame), for permission to get rid of her. Sherman put the officers back in place by telling them, "She outranks me!"

One of the most valuable, but difficult, lesson the best leaders learn is when to restrain their own power. Just because a person is officially in charge, that does not make it automatically right for he or she to exercise that power, especially over professionals who have more knowledge and experience on the subject. Prime Minister Winston Churchill would argue his particular viewpoint for hours with his cabinet members, but if any stood their ground and proposed a different course of action, he would support them.

And there is another lesson that healthcare professionals can learn from the above examples. Anything that benefits our patients' care only serves to strengthen us in the end. Anything that detracts from that position, only ends up hurting us. That is to say, when we participate in, or acquiesce, to policies or procedures that are not in our patients' best interests, we make ourselves and our associates more vulnerable to the intrusion and interference by others. As medical professionals, the first question we should ask ourselves is, "Does this help or hinder the care of our patients?" To the extent that such action does or does not, this should help guide our actions.

Report on the Loss of the "Titanic" (S.S.)

THE MERCHANT SHIPPING ACTS, 1854 to 1906.

IN THE MATTER OF the Formal Investigation held at the Scottish Hall, Buckingham Gate, Westminster, on the 2nd, 3rd, 7th, 8th, 9th, 10th, 14th, 15th, 16th, 17th, 20th, 21st, 22nd, 23rd and 24th May, the 4th, 5th, 6th, 7th, 10th, 11th, 12th, 13th, 14th, 17th, 18th, 19th, 21st, 24th, 25th, 26th, 27th, 28th and 29th June, at the Caxton Hall, Caxton Street, Westminster, on the 1st and 3rd July, and at the Scottish Hall, Buckingham Gate, Westminster, on the 30th July, 1912, before the Right Honourable Lord Mersey, Wreck Commissioner, assisted by Rear-Admiral the Honourable S. A. Gough-Calthorpe, C.V.O., R.N.; Captain A. W. Clarke; Commander F. C. A. Lyon, R.N.R.; Professor J. H. Biles, D.Sc., LL.D., and Mr. E. C. Chaston, R.N.R., as Assessors, into the circumstances attending the loss of the steamship "Titanic," of Liverpool, and the loss of 1,490 lives in the North Atlantic Ocean, in lat. 41° 46' N., long 50° 14' W. on the 15th April last.

REPORT OF THE COURT.

The Court, having carefully enquired into the circumstances of the above mentioned shipping casualty, finds, for the reasons appearing in the Annex hereto, that the loss

of the night the hazy condition of the atmosphere the absence of wind and movement of the sea at and immediately preceding the time of the collision and of the presence of icebergs and fields of ice in the course of the said vessel: that while knowing of the presence of the said ice they failed to alter their course or to diminish their speed so as to avoid the same and failed to provide a sufficient and proper look-out therefor and to supply look-out men with Binoculars: that no adequate lifeboat accommodation was provided on the said Ship having regard to the number of passengers and crew she

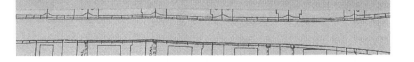

Leadership Lessons From History
Part 2

Title: "That Sinking Feeling"

The first article showed how effective leaders know the limits of their own authority and how healthcare providers can benefit from the goodwill that they have generated, via the care of their patients, in their dialogues with other non-medically-trained stakeholders in the healthcare industry. This example will focus on what happens when leaders ignore or overrule the opinions, greater experience, and knowledge of those directly responsible and in charge of the health, safety and well-being of others.

Much has been written about the circumstances surrounding the sinking of the Titanic on April 15, 1912. The great ship was the very embodiment of the arrogant attitudes of the great captains of industry that had sprung up at the turn of the century. But besides the multiple design and construction flaws that contributed to the disaster, there were two other events that are relevant to our topic.

Anxious to establish a new transatlantic speed record for a passenger vessel right at the start of her maiden voyage, the president of the White Star Line company ordered Captain E. J. Smith to sail full speed ahead. Captain Smith reluctantly followed his boss's order, even though he had received radio messages earlier from other ships in the area warning all vessels that they had spotted icebergs. What neither one knew was that, when they sailed from the English port of Southampton, a middle manager had pulled strings to get on board and had replaced one of the regular ship's officers. This officer vacated the ship so quickly that he failed to hand over the keys to the locked cabinet that held all the binoculars.

In summary, on that ill-fated night, the Titanic hit an iceberg because its perched lookouts did not have a single binocular among them to see the danger in time due to the fact the ship was sailing too fast for the overall conditions. Over a thousand lives were lost because of an event facilitated by the actions of two, non-marine leader-managers whose personal objectives were not tempered by the necessary training and experience to properly judge and balance the safety risks they were assuming.

Any further comment on this lesson would be superfluous, except to say that, after assessing the damage report, the designer of the ship concluded that the magnificent vessel's sinking to the ocean's floor "was inevitable." At the news, Captain Smith's heart certainly sank to the bottom of his pants, which, in all probability, were overflowing already!

Leadership Lessons From History
Part 3-A

Title: "Healthcare Stakeholders Also are Patients"

(Or... A guide to effectively working with an organization's behavioral equivalents to Elizabeth Kubler-Ross' "Five Stages of Grief")

Healthcare professionals have used Elizabeth Kubler-Ross' groundbreaking work on patients' psychological reactions to bad news to help guide patients into accepting having a severe medical or terminal diagnosis. What many physician leaders do not realize is that the same five stages also can be applied to healthcare businesses, corporations, and government offices and their personnel, especially when any of these entities face embarrassing news or difficult choices, as a result of any one of a number of negative disclosures or events.

Table 1: Psychological Reactions to "Bad News"

- Elizabeth Kubler-Ross' "Five Stages of Grief" also can be applied to government offices & businesses as well:
    - Indicted political leaders and cover-ups
    - Major product recalls (e.g. medical devices, pharmaceutical products and drugs)
    - Accidents and disasters, their causes and responses

Table 2: Elizabeth Kubler-Ross' "Five Stages of Grief" are:

- Denial
- Anger
- Bargaining
- Depression
- Acceptance

Physician leaders can help guide non-clinical personnel and representatives through **Elizabeth Kubler-Ross'** "Five Stages of Grief" so that true solutions to healthcare problems are addressed in a timely and satisfactory manner. The same counseling strategies used to assist severely ill patients transition to the acceptance stage also can work with administrative personnel and leaders in other industries.

Leadership Lessons From History
Part 3-B

Title: "Five Stages of a Product Recall"

*(Continuing Part of: **Healthcare Stakeholders Also are Patients** Or... A guide to effectively working with an organization's behavioral equivalents to Elizabeth Kubler-Ross' "Five Stages of Grief" for individuals)*

Let's assume a major manufacturing defect was suspected in a part or a device by the users here in the United States. Let's also assume that a review of the available data showed insufficient cause to alert the appropriate regulatory body, or that the agency's preliminary review failed to detect anything wrong. Nonetheless, your group is still concerned enough to request a meeting with the manufacturer. What might a person expect as a result of the meeting?

Accepting the hypothesis that any organization is capable of responding according to Kubler-Ross' Five Stages of Grief, over a time frame of months to years, the leaders or representatives of the manufacturing company could exhibit one or more of the below behaviors:

DENIAL, ANGER, BARGAINING, DEPRESSION, ACCEPTANCE

Of course, it is also possible for an organization to exhibit multiple behaviors or stages simultaneously. For instance, one part of an organization could be in denial while another part is seeking to gag those whom it perceives as pursuing unfounded claims; an organization also may vehemently deny all allegations in public while vigorously pursuing a private or governmental settlement without actually admitting any wrongdoing. For an organization, the stage of "Depression" may be reflected in a dramatic drop in its revenues or stock prices, or from a major change in its leadership, or from a regulatory agency and/or court decision not in their favor. Still, even at that point, their representatives may pursue multiple strategies; e.g., outwardly decrying the "unfair" judgment while negotiating a reduction in penalties in exchange for withdrawing all appeals.

The next part in this series will focus on the denial aspect to such organizational behavior.

Leadership Lessons From History
Part 3-C

Title: "Denial: The First Stage of a Product Recall"

Or..."If a tree falls in the forest, but no one wants to listen, then what? *(A Continuing Part of: **Healthcare Stakeholders Also are Patients**. Or,... A guide to effectively working with an organization's behavioral equivalents to Elizabeth Kubler-Ross' "Five Stages of Grief")*

Initially, denial is the defense mechanism most likely to be invoked at any encounter with representatives from a company facing possible "bad news" about a device defect (Table 1). "Unconfirmed" information is likely to be suppressed, or not revealed fully to higher leaders in their organization, in the interest of not generating any undue alarm with the stockholders.

Table 1: DENIAL: Expected organizational responses during the initial phase

- "This does not happen to OUR products!"
- "These only are ISOLATED incidences"
- "It only happens in EXTREME circumstances to a few"
- "The number of events has not reached STATISTICAL significance"
- "The data is FAULTY"
- "Proportionally, the numbers are still small... or smaller than (another example)"

These responses may be frustrating to physician leaders. A good analogy of such organizational responses is the "Dead Parrot" skit from the famous British comedy show, "Monty Python's Flying Circus." In the show, the store owner informs the customer that the recently purchased dead parrot was just sleeping. Yet, in examining the past, whether or not it is a potentially defective product, or a new drug with previously unrealized and severe side effects, the "Dead Parrot" skit is repeatedly played out by different players.

An effective strategy to use for such organizational resistance is to point out that, in healthcare, and for the good and the overall best concern of the patients, not acting until there is absolute proof may do more harm than good. The question should be, "Is it safe?" and not "Do we have evidence that it is unsafe." The two statements represent opposite perspectives. The Space Shuttle Challenger disaster happened, in part, because the focus was not on demonstrating that the defective "O" rings were safe, but, rather, because the responsibility to prove that the "O" rings were unsafe was placed on the skeptics. Another way of stating the same question is to remind everyone that the prime medical ethic is, and always shall be this: "First, do no harm."

Leadership Lessons From History
Part 3-D

Title: "The Other Stages of Grief"

Physician leaders can help guide non-clinical personnel and representatives through **Elizabeth Kubler-Ross**' "Five Stages of Grief" so that true solutions to healthcare problems are addressed in a timely and satisfactory manner.

In the previous discussion, "Denial" was shown to be the first defense mechanism typically used by many leaders of organizations facing bad news. Subsequent to that, anger, bargaining, depression and then, finally, the stage of acceptance is reached, but not before potential obstacles are resolved.

After bringing up a particularly difficult issue, physicians may encounter push-back, or even threats to their careers, including legal actions, if they continue to pursue an unpalatable or uncomfortable question or situation, especially if it involves a potential reduction in the organization's finances. Even when confronted with reasonable proof, confirming a physician's suspicion, the organization's leaders often minimize or explain away (bargain down) the impact. In the past, a medical product was re-designed while still selling or utilizing older models and fixing the potentially defective models only if problems developed in people. More recently, a major auto company essentially did the same with a car part.

A decade ago, a major manufacturer of computer chips explained away their corporate decision, not to replace the defective computer chips sold in their consumers' computers, as the chips' discovered mathematical miscalculations occurred only during complex computations, computations that were unlikely to be utilized by the average consumer! The ensuing consumer backlash made them reconsider that position.

Physician leaders can assist other leaders avoid such flawed reasoning by pointing out that, historically, such information is eventually revealed and that the damage to their corporate reputation and goodwill, never mind the legal recoveries, is likely to exceed any short-term monetary setback. Additionally, and depending on the situation and their position, physician leaders should seek out champions within and outside of the organization who can take up the issue for them. Other than that, physician leaders should document all that they have done and their discussions to resolve such issues or problems.

Leadership Lessons From History
Part 3-E, Statements

Title: "Applying Elizabeth Kubler-Ross' Stages"

Healthcare professionals can learn from Elizabeth Kubler-Ross' groundbreaking work on a patient's psychological reactions to "bad health news" to successfully interact with other leaders in or outside the medical profession, especially when those other leaders are facing embarrassing news or financially difficult choices or actions. The following represents typical leadership statements illustrating those stages.

Table 1: DENIAL: Typical organizational statements made during the initial phase of a product recall

- "This does not happen to OUR products!"
- "These only are ISOLATED incidences"
- "It only happens in EXTREME circumstances to a few"
- "The number of events has not reached STATISTICAL significance"
- "The data was FAULTY"
- "Proportionally, the numbers are still small… or smaller than (another example)"

Table 2: ANGER (Blame, Protest & Frustration)

- "It's the CUSTOMER'S fault!"
- "The INSTALLATION was faulty"
- "The MAINTENANCE was faulty"
- "It's the SUPPLIER'S fault!"
- "What is YOUR hidden agenda in making these unsupported allegations?"
- "We will take legal action against anyone or any institution harming the reputation of our product, or business/corporation, or its leaders, by making these false and deleterious accusations."

Table 3: BARGAINING (Positioning)

This includes all lobbying, PAC efforts and legal maneuvering meant to circumnavigate present laws or regulations. This also includes any efforts to thwart official investigations into the subject in order to mitigate or cancel any potential official request for a recall.

- Recall a product, but call it a "mislabeling"
- Recall only some of the product
- Recall, but keep it quiet
- Recall, only if others are blamed
- Recall, only if the company can obtain concessions
- Recall, but with obstacles to compliance
- Stretch out the recall over an extended time period
- Recall, but only if the company and its leaders can get legal protection
- Recall, but only after the annual stockholders' meeting
- STALL! STALL! STALL!

Table 4: DEPRESSION (Confession)

- "The problem was underestimated"
- "Once known, everything reasonable was done"
- "Others have done worse"
- "Previous directives no longer are operational (e.g., Watergate)"
- "We are confident that once everything is settled, that the company's stock price will return to its previously high levels."

Table 5: ACCEPTANCE (Resignation)

- "We will take responsibility, but we were not responsible"
- "Changes already were underway long before the issue became public"
- "Our people were the first to detect and report it"
- "We will fully cooperate with...."
- "We will support legislation to...."
- "Those responsible no longer are with us"
- "Steps have been taken to ensure that this will never happen again in our company." (Repeated several times over the course of many incidences spanning decades.)

Leadership Lessons From History
Part 4

Title: "Alexander's Greatness"

Our West Point Military Academy's instructors teach its young cadets that the most difficult of all battle maneuvers to accomplish successfully is to attack a prepared enemy force from across a river. During his lifetime, Alexander the Great did this twice. At the Battle of Issus, circa 333 B.C., Darius, the King of Persia, not only managed to maneuver his much larger army behind Alexander's smaller Greek forces, but also had his soldiers dig in behind strong, fixed, fortified positions across a river that separated his army from Alexander's men. The disparaging Greek officers had all but given up hope, when Alexander calmly informed them that they would win a great battle that day. And they did.

How often in Medicine do we ignore the obvious, or fail to use all of our faculties and senses in addressing our patients' medical problems? How often do we first consider the psychological position of our patients, our co-workers, or our administrators before acting or speaking? How often do we fall into a rut, treating the same patients with the same medical conditions the same way, over and over again, until we become numbed by the experience? Have you ever felt as if you were sleep-walking through your whole day? Just like Alexander's officers, could you be missing something obvious?

One of the benefits of change is that it tends to wake us up. Old conventions and habits are challenged and altered, forcing us to look at the situation with new eyes. Rather than resisting change, physicians should embrace the opportunity to re-examine their practices and roles; to use the opportunity to grow and learn, and to, perhaps, reconnect with the obvious: you may treat a disease, but care for a patient. It's all about caring for our patients.

So, how did Alexander the Great win this battle? Simple; by not attacking him, the enemy indirectly communicated that they still feared his awesome reputation as a general. And, despite their superiority in numbers of men, they would stand frozen at their spot when confronted. So, he marched most of his men to one end of the Persian battle line and attacked. Having dug in, Darius' army had lost all mobility and stood there and watched as the Greek forces tumbled them down in order, one after the other, just like a row of stacked dominoes!

The moral of the story is that physician leaders not only should study the psychological position of all of the stakeholders in a given situation, but also look for that one point where the maximal leverage will do the most good.

Leadership Lessons From History
Part 5

Title: "High Flying Performance Incentives"

I had a dream once where the administrators of an airline company gathered all of its pilots at a meeting and announced a new series of cost-cutting maneuvers meant to improve the bottom line. Among the many proposals was one to limit the amount of gasoline pumped into each plane to just five hours of flying time. One pilot stood up and said, "I service the Hawaii route and it takes six hours to fly there. What am I supposed to do?" Excusing himself for a moment, the president of the airline company conferred with the rest of his management staff on the stage. At the end of this side-bar discussion, the president returned to the podium and in a strong and confident voice said, "Well then, we suggest that you fly your plane a little faster to get there in time."

As farfetched as this dream may be, it does illustrate a point: even intelligent people can be fooled by their logic, especially when their knowledge and experience is limited. In fact, the more intelligent someone is, the more prone he or she may be to developing nonsensical policies that require a contortionist's skills to maneuver around. In the last few years, how many times have you felt like the above pilot when speaking to a medical insurance representative or a lay person regulator about their rules and regulations? You're not alone. Recently, the overworked and sleep-deprived physicians of Australia petitioned their National Health ministers for relief, only to be told — and I am not making this up — that they should "drink more coffee!"

It's a lazy, cold and silently snowy Saturday morning here in Oscoda, on the north-east side of Michigan. As I'm typing away on my laptop computer, I'm listening to the TV news. One segment is an interview with an American commercial pilot regarding the latest employee performance plan by his company: they would pay the pilots an added incentive if they agreed to fly with less reserve fuel in their planes.*

This is why experienced physician-leaders are needed at every level of healthcare policy making, especially as we debate the subject of reform. It is our role to tell the emperor when he has no clothes.

---

* Facts supported by a subsequent interview on TV News with Captain Chesley Sullenberger III, the courageous airline pilot who made that miraculous emergency landing on the New York City's Hudson river.

Notes

Leadership Lessons From History
Part 6

Title: "Knowledge vs. Understanding"

My wife thinks she is a great cook. Although capable, her years of culinary experience have been limited to mimicry; that is, she copies recipes. One day, I left her to cook the St. Patrick Day's corned beef. "I've never done this before," she said. "Simple," I replied. "Put the meat into a pot of water and cook it for two hours." "But how much water should I use?" She asked. "Just enough to cover the top," I replied, nonchalantly. Hours later I returned to find the pot filled to the top and spilling its watery contents all over the stove. "What happened?" I asked. "I did exactly what you told me to do," my wife replied, defensively. "But, when I put the water in, the meat kept floating to the top. So I added more and more water to make sure it stayed covered, just like you said!"

Abraham Lincoln once stated that, for some men, twenty years of experience just means one year's experience repeated twenty times. How many people have you met that are just like that? They can recite the "Who", "What", "When", and "Where", and may even be able to perform the "How," but do not understand "Why?" This social situation is not unusual in healthcare, where one interacts with people from all different backgrounds. Their years of familiarity with medical terms and clinical information result in a certain degree of knowledge and experience. But, many do not really understand the "why" of it all, especially when it comes to understanding the unpredictable nature of individual human behavior. Yet, if you ask them, just like my wife, they consider themselves to be experts on the subject. The problem is that, without understanding "why," it is impossible to fix things when they go wrong.

So, how do you successfully interact with such a person? My own observation is that confrontation only makes him or her more defensive. Correction often breeds resentment. Even letting things go wrong does not work as the person will blame others. No. The only viable strategy is to lead by example. At every opportunity, stress the importance of needing to understand the "why" of the issue. Emphasize how true learning does not happen until one truly understands, and this comes from a keen sense of awareness, protracted observation and years of disciplined practice, thought and study.

In summary, the true professional not only knows how to do something, but also understands why he or she is doing it. Otherwise, a little bit of knowledge can be a dangerous thing. Indeed.

Leadership Lessons From History
Part 7

Title: "Marching Orders"

For physician leaders participating in policy making activities, there is a lesson well worth remembering. What follows is a slightly fictionalized version of what happened, but its point is well made.

Before the Japanese invaded the Philippines, in the months prior to the outbreak of WWII, the American and Allied armed forces' generals knew that they would not stand a chance against the Imperial Army in open warfare. So, in coordination with the War Department in Washington D.C., military strategists drew up a plan where they would have all the soldiers march to the Bataan peninsula and hole themselves up there until guaranteed help from America arrived with enough ships to evacuate them all.

Sure enough, subsequent military events occurred as predicted and the Philippine forces followed the plan to the letter, except the rescue ships never arrived. When they inquired by radio what happened to all the vessels they were promised, the operator on the other end hesitated for a moment; he then said, "Didn't you guys hear about Pearl Harbor?"

Planning is an essential step in medical operations' management. But even the best of plans cannot foresee all the unexpected events that might occur. That is why flexibility needs to be incorporated into any plan right from the start. This, however, makes some leaders uncomfortable; they do not wish to surrender control, or trust people to make their own decisions. Hence, many plans go to great lengths in specifying every step and action, effectively reducing its subordinates to unthinking robots. Additionally, in failing to list the plan's assumptions, or listing conditions for which it would be inoperable, events are set in motion that are difficult to stop once started. Just like the military example above, their policies and procedures often box themselves in with no room to maneuver or escape!

There is another lesson to be learned from the above historical example, this one for all those who blindly follow such marching orders regardless of the circumstances. According to the book, "Tears in the Darkness: The Story of the Bataan Death March and Its Aftermath", by Michael Norman and Elizabeth Norman, more than 70,000 American and allied soldiers were made prisoners of war as a result of that short-sighted evacuation plan. Ten thousand of them then died in a forced march by the cruel Japanese guards. But that is not all. Before the Bataan troops were left to surrender, General Douglas MacArthur, the previous U.S. commander in the Philippines prior to being smuggled out by P.T. boat, sent them an encouraging message, that troops and planes were "on the way from the United States." It was a lie.

Notes

Leadership Lessons From History
Part 8

Title: "The Game of Golf"

Golf is a great pastime for physicians to adopt as it takes them outdoors and is great exercise if one walks. So appealing is the game that, long ago, the King of England once had to issue a proclamation forbidding his knights from playing as they were neglecting their martial arts training. Nonetheless, to think of Golf as a mere sport is to miss its wider connotations. Golf also provides many lessons on how to conduct one's life and how to lead others. As more physicians assume leadership roles in healthcare, it is well worth reviewing Golf's many management analogies.

Years ago, I read *Leadership Lessons From the Game of Golf, An 18-Hole Course in Leadership,* by Peter Garber (HRD Press, Inc. Amherst, Massachusetts. © 2006). Simply put, your golf grip, your stance, your alignment, your choice of club, your course management strategy, and your attitude, all contribute to a winning score. Translating this into business parlance, keep a firm, but not too tight control on your people, make sure to give them a solid foundation (e.g., training and education), keep them pointed in the right direction, give them the right tools to do their job, outline a clear but simple work strategy for them to follow, and keep things "light." Uptight employees are not very productive workers. But the most important lesson of all was one single advice: "Keep your eye on the ball!"

As we get caught up in the day-to-day affairs and the many small brush fires that erupt at work all the time, how often do we neglect to remind ourselves of the bigger picture? How often do we lose sight of the "ball?" How many employees can recite the office's Vision and Mission Statements? Do you even have one? Whenever the executive team contemplates a major decision affecting the entire organization, does anyone cross-check them against these guiding operational principles?

As hinted at in this column, the game of Golf has many lessons to teach. However, there is one bit of advice I would give that was not in the book. At the end of the "18-holes," that is to say after a major project has been implemented at work, sit down and tally up all that was gained and lost along the way. Next, check to see how other organizations have done with similar assignments. Then ask yourself this question: "Did your management team shoot par or better?"

Notes

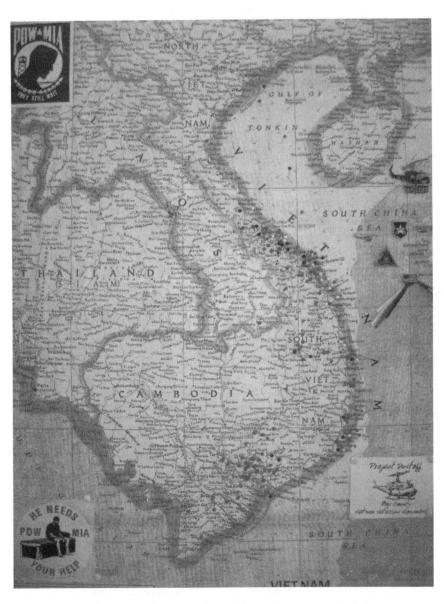

Photo of the map reproduced out of courtesy of Steven H. Berge. Historic Presentations: American Military History. Taken in summer of 2015 as part of the Vietnam Traveling Wall Display, Oscoda, Michigan.

Leadership Lessons From History
Part 9

Title: "The Truth About Healthcare Reform"

When I was in the 8th grade, my Civics teacher promised to give an "A" to any student who came up with a winning strategy for the war in Vietnam.

Taking up the challenge, I spent my evenings and weekends at the Plainfield, N.J., library pouring over everything I could about the subject; I even used my saved up allowance to buy a large map of North and South Vietnam so that I could plot out all the strategic positions. After hours of study, I concluded that the best we could do was a draw; we might even lose!

I wrote out my report and submitted it; a week later I received it back — marked with a big "C+" grade on it. Disappointed, I approached the teacher and told him that I thought I deserved a better grade. I still remember his words. He said, "I asked for a WINNING strategy, not a LOSING one!"

Years later, former Secretary of Defense Robert McNamara admitted that he had come to the same conclusion, at about the same time that I did as a teenager, but he did not have the fortitude to tell President Johnson his opinion.

The truth is that, psychologically, the people of this nation are not yet ready for a truthful, honest, respectful, and open debate on healthcare reform. Just like the above example, many do not even wish to consider other possibilities and will degrade those with a different viewpoint or solution that does not support their wants. Until our attitude changes, the United States will keep going around in circles over its healthcare crisis — and costs! But there is yet another darker truth: no matter what healthcare reform is adopted eventually, special interests will sabotage all intentions and efforts.

I wonder if that teacher ever gave my Civics report a second thought?

THE UNIVERSITY OF MISSISSIPPI MEDICAL CENTER
2500 North State Street
JACKSON, MISSISSIPPI 39216

School of Medicine
Department of Physiology and Biophysics

Area Code 601
362-4411

Mr. Calvin J. Maestro, Jr.
74 Grove Street
North Plainfield, NJ 07060

Dear Calvin:

Thank you for this opportunity to speak for a moment to your graduating Medical Class of 1979.

On the other hand, I do not really know what I would say to my son or daughter upon graduation from medical school. I have already had four sons to graduate from medical school and will have a daughter to graduate this year. And I don't think that any one of them really wanted me to say anything, for each already knew his plans for the future. But if he had wanted me to speak, perhaps I would have suggested a few basic essentials: First, arrange your medical life so that you can enjoy it. Medicine is a beautiful field of knowledge and can be enjoyed immensely under appropriate conditions. On the other hand, when a medical practice is not organized properly, without sufficient time to study and think and to treat your patients properly, it can become a horrendous chore. Each person has to choose his own way to prevent this from happening, but it is most important.

Second, work as much as possible toward organizing medicine for maximum benefit with the least effort and least cost. Unfortunately, with government intrusion into medicine comes great numbers of rules and regulations that vastly increase the physician's work load but without necessarily increasing his effectiveness. Many of the regulations appear because of abuses of the system perpetrated by the physician himself. The less these abuses, the less will be the regulations. But aside from government intrusion, there are ways of organizing medical practice that can be less wasteful of time. For instance, what is the sense of having an office far from one's hospital? Or what is the sense of being far from a source of drugs or of being far from appropriate laboratory facilities? And, can you work in a cooperative way with other doctors so that patients are not necessarily shuffled in an endless succession from doctor to doctor?

Medicine is going to change vastly in the next few years. With leadership from the doctors themselves, a better product will be delivered.

Thank you again for this privilege of speaking, though I know full well that each of you has probably already chosen a course that makes your future rather immutable.

Yours sincerely,

Arthur C. Guyton, M.D.
Chairman and Professor

ACG:bjh

Leadership Lessons From History
Part 10

Title: "Teaching Common Sense"

My expectation of sleeping late in the morning on Saturday was interrupted when my wife dashed into the bedroom asking me to get out of bed and fix the downstairs television. It seems that a special presentation show on a cable television channel had turned black on our T.V. screen. Approaching the situation logically, I tested each of the electronic components: the T.V. set, the cable box, and the VCR. Each one was operating normally. In fact, while all the other cable channels were being received as expected, this one cable channel my wife wanted to tape was blank! A quick check of our upstairs television showed the same situation.

The cable company's service representative answered our telephone call promptly. I explained our situation and told her that the only logical explanation had to be a problem with their central cable feed. The odds of two cable boxes or two television sets malfunctioning on the same single cable channel were extremely remote. "That's impossible," she replied. "If that were the case, we would have had more complaints!" (Maybe, we <u>were</u> the very first couple to complain?)

After my appeal to the cable representative's sense of logic fell on deaf ears, we proceeded to go through her company's set of standardized, customer operational instructions. Nothing worked. Eventually, we ended up making an appointment for a service man to come to our home. My wife was furious. Four hours later, the missing channel reappeared, as if by magic, all by itself.

For eight years I taught a wide array of undergraduate and graduate university courses. My assessment is that, while we do a fine job of asking students to memorize and then recite back what they were taught — we even emphasize research, teamwork and cooperation by having them hand in and orally present project after project — what we have not done well is to make sure our students can think, to approach problems logically and systematically.

All too often the first explanation that comes to mind is accepted as truth without further exploration of the issue or confirmation; or, if confirmation is sought, only those findings in support of the convenient hypothesis is accepted, the rest ignored or trivialized. I have seen this phenomenon at work even in corporate executive meetings and in medical researchers. The fact that many intelligent men and women have gone along with such nonsensical proclamations only pinpoints the degree of work needed to correct such wayward thinking. It's also the likely reason why, in this country, common sense is becoming rarer every day.

Notes

Leadership Lessons From History
Part 11

Title: "Trust but Verify"

If it had not been for the following event, the world may not have heard of Ulysses S. Grant; the U.S. even might not have won the American Civil War.

In the first few years of the War of Northern Aggression, the North had little to celebrate by way of military success. This all was about to change in 1863 as General William Starke Rosecrans and his Union Army of the Cumberland repeatedly drove his opposing Confederate forces back – until they met in what was to be a final showdown in a heavily wooded area called Chickamauga, near Chattanooga, Tennessee. Success there for the Union could result in the South losing its whole western theater of battle.

Expecting the Confederates to make a desperate fight against them, General Rosecrans deployed his men in a defensive live, only to have an officer ride up to headquarters and announce that he had just come from the front and a whole section of the line was undefended; the implication being that the federal troops assigned to cover that section had gotten lost in the forest along the way.

Immediately, General Rosecrans gave the order for all adjoining units to spread out and cover the gap in the line. As luck would have it, just as the blue troops were moving, the Confederates attacked and drove the Union Army back. Subsequently, and after the embarrassing defeat, General Rosecrans was reassigned to a lesser post.

Ironically, it was later discovered that the unnamed Union officer had been wrong; the "missing" Union troops indeed were at their assigned position in the line, but the bush was so heavy that he had missed seeing them!

As physicians we are repeatedly confronted with updated news, reports or alerts regarding our patients and our medical practices from our co-workers, our administrators, health care insurers, and from respected medical journals. Many of these sources we trust implicitly. However, before acting on any news, it would do physicians well to remember the words of our past president, Ronald Reagan: "Trust, but verify." It is something that General Rosecrans likely regretted not doing for the rest of his life.

Leadership Lessons From History
Part 12

Title: "Remember the Alamo"

Many years ago, my family and I visited the historic Fort Alamo in San Antonio, Texas. Inside the church chapel, in one of the side displays, was a listing of all the men who stood and fought against General Santa Anna and his 1500 Mexican soldiers in 1836. Motioning for my wife to come over, I said to her, proudly, "Look at this; out of the 180 or so defenders of the Alamo, there were seven doctors, but only three lawyers!" Without missing a beat, my wife replied, "That's because the lawyers were smarter."

As a rule, most doctors consider themselves to be intelligent men and women. Yet, as any con-man can tell you, they can be the most gullible of marks. One reason for it is that we are trained to believe our patients, unless they give us a reason to doubt them. Another, is because we've entered a humanitarian oriented profession where we subscribe to the general belief that all men and women are intrinsically good – "Evil" is the patient's disease or the malady, and we're the good guys!

Although there may be a patient here and there that might be exaggerating or faking his symptoms for secondary monetary gain or attention, we consider such incidences to be exceptions to the rule, rather than usual environment or expected behavior. Yet, such selfish gains and purposeful lies are regularly encountered in political and business fields; the entertainment industry and its people, as a whole, are in a class by themselves regarding scandals. Which brings me to my point.

The real history of the Alamo is that the defenders never planned on getting trapped. They underestimated Santa Anna's rapid military response and were caught off guard by the quick marching Mexican soldiers. The Texans were fighting for independence; the Mexicans were fighting for retention of their sovereign land. Often, in real life, "Right" and "Wrong" become blurred, depending on "which side of the Rio Grande you're on." And that is what physicians should remember before advocating a position that traps the profession up against a wall where they have no viable options left.

Postscript: I'd like to think that the other "missing" American lawyers at the Alamo were out there trying to negotiate a truce.

Notes

Leadership Lessons From History
Part 13

Title: "The Difference Between Accountability and Responsibility"

Just before the battle of Bull Run (a.k.a., Manassas) in 1861, the first major land battle of the American Civil War, and during the planning stage, the medical director of the Union Army asked to have the drivers of the ambulance wagons transferred to the medical corps' direct command. The army commander refused his request; the same drivers and wagons were needed to move supplies to the battle; they then could be used to evacuate the wounded later on. The doctor accepted the decision of his superiors, except the battle did not go as planned. Instead, the Union Army was routed soundly and had to flee. In the panicked retreat that followed, the regular army officers commandeered the wagons and its drivers for their own men.

Without any means of transporting the wounded back to Washington, D.C., many injured soldiers suffered for days on end, prostrate on the spent battlefield in the middle of a hot summer. Quite a few died who otherwise could have been saved. In the public outcry that ensued, the Army's Surgeon General, Clement A. Finley, was relieved of his duties despite forty years of dutiful service.

As physicians and other health provider personnel are asked to assume ever increasing management roles, it is well worth remembering this story. In the above example, the responsible army commander's refusal to grant official leadership of the ambulance drivers to the medical branch was the root cause of the evacuation disaster. Nonetheless, the military doctors were made accountable for the mistake. This is the difference between responsibility and accountability. Always ask yourself, "If something goes wrong, who's going to pay?" If it is you, then you'd better be the one responsible for making the decisions.

MICROBIAL CHEMISTRY RESEARCH FOUNDATION
INSTITUTE OF MICROBIAL CHEMISTRY

14-23, KAMIOSAKI 3-CHOME, SHINAGAWA-KU, TOKYO, JAPAN. TELEGRAMS: [MICROBCHEM, TOKYO] TEL: (441) 4173-4

October 16, 1978

Mr. Calvin Maestro Jr.
Editor of the Journal
74 Grove St.
North Plainfield, N. J. 07060
U. S. A.

Dear Mr. Maestro:

    I found your letter just after I came back from two weeks travelling.

    I write the following short letter:

"Progress in sciences of diseases and development of more effective treatment modi are dependent on you; be a person of spirit and kind to patients and keep you in high level of medical sciences with a high philosophy."

                                Sincerely yours,

                                Hamao Umezawa
                                Director

HU/tn

Leadership Lessons From History
Part 14

Title: "True Visionary Leadership"

This is a more recent history lesson for all physicians who have leadership responsibilities: either direct or indirect, whether or not as doctors you have staff reporting to you, or just have a reverence leadership position within your organization.

The late Kotaku Wamura was a ten-term mayor of the Japanese city of Fudai. In the 1970s he used his considerable political influence to put through the construction of a fifty-foot floodgate to protect the city from a tsunami.

Similar to the acquisition of Alaska by the United States from Russia in 1867, called "Seward's folly," as the purchase was championed by the then serving United States Secretary of State William H. Seward, critics of the Japanese mayor and his wall balked at both the unnecessary size and cost of the project.

Nonetheless, at great risk to his political career and personal prestige, Mayor Wamura persisted. In 1987 the floodgate was completed. The rest, as they say is history. On March 11, 2011, the city of Fundai survived the terrible tsunami that devastated much of the rest of the region — all because the floodgate was high enough to stop the surging waters!

As any fan of the comic book hero, Spider-Man can recite, "With great power, comes great responsibility." In building the tsunami wall, Mr. Wamura demonstrated several of the personal traits of great leaders: vision and the courage to see it through. The only other historical example that comes to mind is the construction of the Panama Canal by President Theodore Roosevelt. Without the Panama Canal, the U.S. would have had a much more difficult time winning the Pacific Theater during WWII.

I cannot help but wonder if, in the post-war years in Japan, when he first became mayor of Fudai, Mr. Wamura drew strength from Bill and Theodore's examples of leadership? He certainly did not live long enough to see his great work vindicated.

Reference:

Hosaka, Tomoko A. *How one Japanese village defied the tsunami*. Associated Press online. 5/13/11.

Notes

VETERANS ADMINISTRATION
HOSPITAL
130 WEST KINGSBRIDGE ROAD
BRONX, NEW YORK 10468

September 12, 1978

IN REPLY
REFER TO:

526/115

Calvin J. Maestro, Jr.
Editor , EMDNJ-NJMS Yearbook
74 Grove Street
North Plainfield, NJ 07060

Dear Mr. Maestro:

Enclosed is a short letter in response to your request.

Sincerely yours,

Rosalyn S. Yalow, Ph.D.
Senior Medical Investigator, VA

Enclosure

Society has made an enormous investment in your medical education. You and your family have also invested time and money as well as blood, sweat and tears. At this time you should appreciate that this investment is justified not on the basis of financial return but rather on your willingness and enthusiasm in dedicating yourself to the service of man. The ways to serve are many - for some it will be private practive, for others academic medicine - there will be specialists and generalists. Which way you choose depends on your personality and interests. All are equally meritorious. However, whatever your choice, dedicate yourself to excellence to the limits of your competence and to integrity.

Leadership Lessons From History
Part 15

Title: "Leadership Success vs. Ethics"

All too often, either in the movies or on television, or even through personal experience watching others, the forfeiture of any personal set of morals or ethics is considered the standard price to pay for success if a person aspires to achieve a high leadership position in life. Proof of this resides in the prevailing assumption in this country that *we expect our politicians to lie to us* whenever the situation calls for it. As cynical as this attitude may be, it only admits what many of us already believe.

Whether or not it is political spin, propaganda, or outright lying to protect one's reputation, too many of our leaders place greater emphasis on priorities other than telling the truth. In part, this is due to the modern, commonly held, relativistic moral attitude that there no clear right or wrong on any issue; or due to a utilitarian viewpoint, which states that any action can be justified as long as it benefits the most people. It is almost as if some people never understood the U.S. Constitutional Amendments, which were enacted in part to protect individuals against incursions perpetrated by a popular majority, or by a wayward government.

In short, too many of our leaders, and our people as well, subscribe to the philosophy that the end does indeed justify the means, and that if the situation calls for it, it is OK to lie. This stand is not far from the one taken by evil men a generation ago to justify the genocide of a whole ethnic race. Or used by the supporters of one political party to break into the Washington, D. C. campaign office of their main opponent, and then later covered up by even the President of the United States.

Therefore, it was with some surprise that I recently was watching a late-night television series regarding an ancient kingdom and saw a main character of the story resign his position, at great personal risk to himself and to his family, rather than carry out the king's unethical command. I also was reminded of one's state's supreme court ruling, which allowed employers to fire an at-will employee, for no cause and on the spot, if he or she refused to carry out a clearly illegal order on the company's behalf. Did Congress really intend to pass a federal law that supported or even indirectly encouraged criminal business activities? Were all other laws prohibiting illegal acts suddenly nullified? I doubt it. But, then again, I'm no lawyer.

Leadership Lessons From History
Part 16

Title: "Trust & the Horror of Infectious Diseases"

I am lucky to have been born in the last half of the Twentieth Century. Through the world's progress in medicine, I was protected in childhood from long-time diseases, such as polio, tetanus, pertussis and diphtheria. I took the swine flu shot in the 1970s while in medical school in New Jersey. I received the Hepatitis B series as soon as it was available. A yearly flu shot not only protects me, but also protects my patients. To understand my motivation, all one needs to do is read a little history.

Today's people have forgotten the sheer horror that a transmittable infectious disease can cause in a community. They have no first-hand experience seeing how quickly these microscopic terrors can ravage the body of a young child or infant onto death itself. Even as late as the 1950s, the news of a polio outbreak in a major city could stop it cold. A smallpox outbreak was so detrimental to the survival of a small community that, back in the late 1700s, bands of men would abduct any adult refusing to be (crudely) immunized and subject him or her to the vaccination despite the high risks (by our standards) of death. Even back then they knew the value of herd immunity. During the great influenza pandemic of 1918, in a few days' train ride, hundreds of young soldiers on their way to war became sick when packed closely together in railroad boxes; many of them dying abysmal deaths from the flu. Another example: There is a very good reason why Central Park in New York City has a statue dedicated to the memory of an animal – Balto – the canine who helped lead a dog sled team to an isolated town in wintry Alaska, delivering diphtheria antitoxin preparations to desperately sick children.

This is the real tragedy behind the decision by so many modern and progressive mothers these days to forgo immunizing their children; not only are they rejecting the benefits of modern medicine for their child, but they are also rejecting civilized society itself. During the American

Civil War, so many new young recruits immediately became sick as soon as they arrived in military camp, with childhood diseases they had missed while growing up in isolated communities, that one commander refused to take any more until they had "matured." Swapping the risk of childhood immunization with the risk of their progeny acquiring the actual disease years later is a very poor health tradeoff indeed. The measles and pertussis outbreaks currently in the United State are just a hint of what could appear in the future.

But there is an even sadder end to this story. According to one study, too many healthcare providers do not routinely take the yearly flu shot. Recently, this issue has been elevated into a legal battle between mandatory workplace requirements for its healthcare personnel and an individual's private right to choose. Nonetheless, the main underlying question has not been addressed openly: Why have so many people lost their faith and trust in modern medicine? What's ironic is that many of these people are willing to try alternative and complementary medical products or therapies, even when it comes from unreliable sources. What does that say about the situation: A lack of public trust.

Public trust is why everyone involved in Medicine needs to practice and uphold the highest standards of professional integrity and ethics. Everyone, from the vaccine makers and the medical device and pharmaceutical companies, to the vitamin and compounding manufacturers, to the government watchdog agencies and regulators responsible for their oversight, to our medical universities and biological labs, and our hospitals performing patient studies and the quality review organizations working with them, from the pharmacist, physical therapist and all the way to the specialist's or local primary care provider's office, we all need to be responsible for one another's health care practices and behaviors.

Every report of a covered up laboratory mistake, drug or medical device recall, or of falsified and manipulated data in medical studies, or of hired ghost writers being utilized secretly to write biased reports favorable to one manufacturer's product, or of drug approval reviews being performed by appointed panels whose members have clear financial conflicts of interest, or of doctors operating on the wrong extremity, or of clinics not cleaning their endoscopes properly, or of healthcare workers (no matter where in the world, and in their misguided belief that the overall health benefits outweigh the risks) economizing by reusing unsterilized needles, or of healthcare workers being arrested by a sheriff for properly reporting the non-professional behavior of a hospital's physician, and then having that hospital fire the workers in retribution, these unethical acts, singularly and collectively, undermine the whole healthcare profession, just like a cancer gnawing at the bones of our medical infrastructure.

There is a dialogue in the movie, "Glory" that is the perfect ending for this piece. In the movie, a film about the first all-black regiment in the Union Army during the American Civil War, the Academy-Award winning actor, Daniel Washington, addresses the Coronel, played by Matthew Broderick. Referring to the sad tragedy that most wars are, Daniel says, "We're all dirty. But we can come out of this clean." Sage advice for all those involved in healthcare: we need to come clean.

Leadership Lessons From History
Part 17

Title: "Of Silos and System's Operational Performance"

Imagine you are the newly appointed manager over a particular segment of a long assembly line in a complex company. Imagine also that you have done a risk analysis and concluded that the previous leader had allowed certain key repairs to lapse on the machinery running your part of the assembly line. Although these two particular pieces were still performing according to specifications, your intimate knowledge of the parts led you to conclude that it was just a matter of time before each piece failed. Further analysis showed that the whole assembly line would need to be shut down for three days while either one was being replaced. Taking pro-active command of the situation, you order the two replacement parts.

The very next month both assembly line pieces fail. As you already had the parts available, the technical people were able to install both during the line's routinely scheduled minor maintenance downtime, without any interruption being noticed by either of the managers in front or behind your segment. However, imagine your surprise when, at the next budget meeting, you are called on the carpet by the accounting department for exceeding the company's monthly budgetary expectations for your segment of the assembly line!

The above example illustrates the constant, at-odds tensions that exist in some organizations between fixed, individual silo performance expectations and overall system's organizational outcomes. However, there is another aspect to the story that often goes unnoticed. Several years ago two managers of a company were caught purposely manufacturing crisis situations at work just so that they could jump in with saving solutions to the very problems they created behind the scenes. The two managers explained that this was the only way they knew to get recognized and promoted from within; that is to say, if a manager did a great job and kept problems from happening in the first place, his or her performance was taken for granted by the company. In the example cited at the beginning of this example, if the leaders had done a root-cause analysis, they would have found fault with the previous manager and praised the current one.

Lesson: Until your organization — including the office — routinely rewards employees for thinking and acting according to what is operationally best from an outcome-based, system's viewpoint, your people are likely going to just wait until something bad happens.

Leadership Lessons From History
Part 18

Title: "The Great Mouse Hunt"

I arrived home late one night after a busy day at the office. Exhausted, I just wanted to rest. Instead, at the door, I was greeted by my upset wife and my four-year-old son, who was dressed up as the movie fighter "Rambo." "There's a mouse in the basement," she said. "And I want you to march right down there and catch it before it ruins all of our belongings!"

Promising that I would take a look, I went to the bathroom to splash some cold water on my face. Along the way, David repeatedly tugged at my shirt, saying, "Come on Dad, we've got to go down the basement and shoot the mouse!" Fed up, I grabbed his plastic rifle and said, "David! This is a toy gun. It shoots toy bullets. And that is a real live mouse down there!" Giving me a look that clearly indicated that my son did not believe how dumb his father was, David sighed and said, "If we go downstairs and make lots of noise, the mouse will run away." Mouse Psychology 101, from a four-year-old!

Confrontation is inevitable in life. Physicians often find themselves caught up in these interpersonal relationship problems at work. But, there are better ways of handling such situations than others. Understanding the psychological state of the other person is useful. So is humor. When David was a teenager, he once worked as a sales clerk in a video store. Spotting a kid trying to steal a game by putting it inside his sweat shirt, my son approached the perpetrator, looked him straight in the eye, and said, "How long have you been doing this?" Embarrassed, the guy put the video game back and immediately left the store.

In direct, one-on-one meetings, always start out by emphasizing the person's good points and previous positive contributions. Clearly communicate that you are willing to work with him or her to resolve the issue and that, while you respect a differing viewpoint, you do not necessarily agree with it nor believe that approach to be beneficial for the rest of the team. Sometimes, just offering an empathetic ear to the other person is enough to make everyone feel better.

As to the end of the story, David and I went downstairs to the basement and yelled and screamed and ran around, making as much noise as we possibly could. At the end, I emerged from the encounter completely rejuvenated. I even gave my wife a big kiss on the lips. We never saw that mouse again.

Notes

McGill University

Department of Anatomy
Strathcona Anatomy and Dentistry Building

September 20, 1978

Calvin Maestro Jr.
76 Grove Street
North Plainfield
New Jersey 07060

Dear Mr. Maestro:

In answer to your request to write a short letter to my son or daughter upon graduation, I enclose such a letter.

Yours sincerely,

(C.P. Leblond)

C. P. Leblond

CPL:cl
Enclosure

Postal address: 3640 University Street, Montreal, PQ, Canada H3A 2B2

To a son or daughter:

The main problem in the life of a doctor is to be more than a repair man. Few can follow in the footsteps of creators like Osler and Penfield. Many can add a new dimension to their practice through sympathy, understanding and guidance.

Sympathy comes easily when you are happy, but let it come even when you are not.

Understanding begins with understanding yourself, from how the body functions to how the mind reaches idealistic aspirations; grows by listening to others, both at home and in your office; and finally by getting to know those who, like Dostoievsky and Proust, have been scrutinized men.

If to sympathy and understanding, you can add a sense of duty, you will be able to give guidance to those who need it.

Then you will be not just a repair man, but also a builder and a force in your community.

Leadership Lessons From History
Part 19

Title: "On EHR Form, Function & Purpose. Or, Still Waiting for Godot"

Every time I work with a new electronic health record (EHR), I am reminded of the story of the Hawker Hurricane monoplane in WWII. Along with the Supermarine Spitfire, this single seat fighter plane was responsible for shooting down so many German Nazi warplanes in the summer of 1940 that it won the Battle of Britain, thereby saving England from invasion. However, the Hurricane did have a problem.

As with most projects, the economically focused development of the Hawker Hurricane represented a culmination of design compromises from as many existing plans as possible. One of these compromises included the seating of a fuel tank directly in front of the pilot's instrument panel. Undoubtedly, this design facet solved many aeronautical problems. But they forgot the plane's wartime purpose!

Similarly, Electronic health record (EHR) computer programs are very different from standard administrative or business-type counterparts. EHR programs need to be utilized by medical personnel across a wide array of clinical settings having direct patient contact; often, this involves operating in several geographically distinct places simultaneously. The direct access to and recording of new medical information also needs to flow seamlessly from nurse to physician and then back again without a whole stream of keyboard clicks or prompts effectively acting as time-delaying barriers to the operators. Sadly, even in this day and age, that is not the case.

Why does it require the purchase of several operating licenses if the same physician has a computer open in each of three patient exam rooms? Why are each of the day's patient hospital progress note entries by the nurse, the doctor, and others, separated into their own files, which then require the viewer to open and close each in turn? Why don't all of the EHR programs "talk" to one another? How many times have you felt like the EHR program was "fighting" your attempts to input or extract clinically vital patient information? Why is it that, despite it being a decade since JAMA (March 9, 2005) published its editorial, *Waiting for Godot*, are computer programmers and EHR dealers still making medical personnel *adopt to the machine* rather than the other way around?

The Hawker Hurricane's prime purpose was to go to war. That is to say, while one does not expect to be shot at while flying a civilian plane, the reverse is true in a warplane. All it took was single, red-hot tracer bullet from an enemy machine gun hitting the fuel tank of a Hawker Hurricane, and its pilot was immediately immersed in flames. Remember this story the next time you get burnt by an EHR!

Leadership Lessons From History
Part 20

Title: "Herd Mentality & Group Think"

When I was a Pre-Med student in college, I accepted my counselor's strong advice to sign up for an advanced mathematics course in my junior year of college. Half-way through the mathematics course, I knew I had made a mistake. While I held onto a respectable B+ grade, it seemed that I always was one step behind while other students in the same class were breezing along with 90+ marks on all their quizzes.

On the day after our mid-term exam, the professor declared that this was the best class he had ever taught and that he was going to abandon the regular curriculum and introduce us to the real math — the secret math only for the very worthy. He then announced that everything we had been taught about mathematics was WRONG! To prove his point, he was going to show us that ONE equaled ZERO.

At first we laughed, but the professor then proceeded to write out a long, mathematical proof that did show that one equaled zero. We were stunned. He had proven the impossible. The teacher then asked the class, "Now, who still does not believe that one equals zero?" Only a foreign student from Norway and I raised our hands. Again, he went through the entire mathematical proof just for the two of us. Neither one of us budged. This made the professor angry. "I want to see the two of you right after class!" He said.

The hallway bell then rang, signaling the end of the class. One at a time, the other students walked passed us. I heard them whisper, "Dummies!" Shortly, we were alone with the teacher. During the interval, I berated myself for being so stubborn, knowing that my future career as a doctor was gone. But then the professor's frown turned into a smile. He squatted down, looked at us, and said, "Just keep up the good work and I will guarantee you both an A." The last half of the math course was impossible. Even our best students fell by the wayside. But, in the end, that Norwegian student and I received our A grades.

Physician leaders can take a lesson from the above. Although we often are accused of not understanding the administrative, insurance, financial, legal and technological side of the practice of medicine, we're experts at feeling what's natural or not. We're also independent thinkers; we do not always agree with a higher authority's viewpoint. This tendency can be threatening to those accustomed to automatic allegiance. The story also points out how even intelligent people can be tripped up by their own logic; the professor's abstract mathematical theorem indeed was correct, but that did not make it right. Nonetheless, most in the class accepted it as true. The same phenomena happens with group think or herd mentality; it is too easy to go along with the crowd. It turns out that, in the end, common sense is not that common at all.

Leadership Lessons From History
Part 21

Title: "The Value of Stable Teamwork"

At the 2008 Summer Olympics in Peking, China, the U.S. Track and Field coaches — both on the men's and women's teams — had a dilemma. For the 4 X 100 meter relay races, they could either go with the team of four runners that got them to the finals, or substitute a number of these athletes with their best track stars who had been competing in the individual races that had been run so far.

Since both the men's and the woman's U.S. teams were heavily favored to win the gold medal, the coaches knew that anything less would be construed as a failure on their part. That is to say, their coaching careers were going to be determined by the outcome of this one race. Unwilling to stake their future using second-string runners, both the men's and women's U.S. Track and Field coaches opted to substitute some of the current runners with the individual star athletes for the finals.

Both teams lost the Gold Medal. In fact, neither the men's nor woman's teams won a single medal. With little time to practice their handoffs, both newly-formed teams dropped the batons in the middle of the races.

The race does not always go to the swiftest, or to the most talented. Teamwork is essential for success and this requires consistency in personnel. It takes time and experience to develop successful relationships. These qualities are not automatically interchangeable. Quality-of-care studies have shown that a critical step in Medicine is the "handoff" of the patient by the hospitalist to the office provider. <u>Too many patient "handoffs" invite team members to "drop the baton"</u> Frequent handoffs also make patients feel as if no single person is caring for them. HENCE, a key question that should be asked during the finalization of any medical or administrative decision should be…

"Are we placing the patient first?"

To the extent that this does or does not happen, the answer to this question becomes the defining factor whether or not an institution is truly "patient centered."

Leadership Lessons From History
Part 22

Title: "Outcomes are Related to Process as Effectiveness is to Efficiency"

One day at sea, the first mate came to the captain with the morning's report. "First, the ship's engines are operating at peak efficiency. Second, the results of our employee satisfaction survey are in and our sailors' morale has never been higher. Third, of 1,000 shipboard instruments, only one is malfunctioning." "That's great," said the captain. "We'll get a great bonus once we reach port. When do we arrive?" "I don't know," answered the first mate. "Our ship's compass is broken."

As more physicians become involved with the operations of their clinics, it is well to remember the difference between efficiency and effectiveness. The above story illustrates how a business can succeed at being efficient while still failing to be effective. For example, how can all of the officers and managers of a financial institution deserve a bonus if the bank failed where they worked? Unfortunately, many of the performance indicators used to determine advancement concentrate on improvements in production or in processes while utilizing the same (or less) amount of resources (efficiency) rather than for improving outcome. Outcome is where the tire meets the road.

Similarly, many of the quality indicators in healthcare concentrate on process rather than outcome. Only a handful of many medical quality measures actually are outcome oriented. This is why more outcome studies are needed in healthcare. Not only do we need to know how fast we are spinning our medical wheels, but also in what direction and how well our passengers are doing.

There is another management lesson to be learned. In their drive to increase production, leaders can inadvertently institute a negative feedback loop where they reward less efficient units at the cost of those who are better. The result is that employees work at the most minimal level tolerated since their reward for any increase in their efforts is to be given more work to perform!

Notes

August 13, 1987

Calvin J. Maestro, Jr., M.D.
Jones Clinic
One Ten Ridge Road
Munster, Indiana 46321

Dear Dr. Maestro:

Thank you for your letter of August 4. No mistake was made. Verapamil is generally thought not to cause sexual dysfunction, but sexual dysfunction associated with taking verapamil has been reported.

Sincerely,

Mark Abramowicz, M.D.

MA/msa

Leadership Lessons From History
Part 23

Title: "Garbled Transmission"

"Black Sea researchers discovered an undersea river in England with waterfalls and rapids"

A recent headline proclaimed. Then the article stated, "Researchers have discovered a river flowing along the bottom of the Black Sea. The undersea river contains channels and researchers discovered it near the Black Sea in England." Furthermore, the reviewer stated, "The existence of this undersea river is due to the much saltier Mediterranean Sea flowing into the Black Sea through the Bosporus Strait."

Physician leaders need to be aware of the constant struggle in communicating effectively their medical terminology and information to others and the perceived need and desire by associates, often within the same organization, to simplify that communication as it may be released to the public. Often, the resulting watered-down article is as nonsensical as a headline proclaiming England as being geographically near the Black Sea!

To prevent such misunderstandings, the physician leader needs to ask, "Who will be conducting the interview? And, "Who will be writing or editing the article? What are his/her credentials? Does the person have the knowledge and experience to truly understand the issues? Is their training both broad and deep enough to appreciate the complexities?" Lastly, "Will I be able to review and edit the piece before it is released?

If the answers to the above questions are not satisfactory, the physician leader should either decline to make a comment, or petition for editorial control of their own communication pieces.

In the movie, "Armageddon," where a spaceship was being launched to save the earth from an incoming asteroid, it was more effective to teach the men of a deep-sea oil drilling team how to be astronauts than to teach astronauts how to drill. Similarly, news organizations, or communication units, should employ or utilize medically experienced personnel and train them to be good writers than to take someone who majored in English Literature and ask them to translate medical subjects.

Source:

From: http://www.newsoxy.com/science/undersea-river-discovered-black-sea-14070.html

Leadership Lessons From History
Part 24

Title: "Adopting Business Ethics"

Over a decade ago, when healthcare quality data reporting was still in its early stages, a director of one of the big three U.S. auto companies confronted me about the lack of detailed reporting in the medical profession. He pointed out that, in his business, they could track a single nut or bolt all the way from the manufacturer to the product in which it was installed. He ended his point by saying, "I wish you doctors would adopt better business practices." I gazed at the auto executive and, with a smile on my face, I replied to his challenge by saying, "I tell you what I will do. I will get every doctor in this nation to adopt better business practices if, on the other hand, they also can adopt your business ethics."

My reply caught the auto executive by surprise. I could see his mind was processing what I had said. Then, with a sigh, he whispered, "OH GOD NO!"

I once listened to an author in an audio tape speak about how there was no such thing as "Business Ethics." His point was that the same ethical principles should apply to everyone, no matter what his or her occupation or profession. In addition, and since that time, I have come to my own conclusion: if it is not a conflict between two moral imperatives, it is not an "ethical dilemma." It is something else. What often passes for an ethical dilemma is merely the unpleasant feeling of needing to make a clear choice between a selfish interest, want or desire, and something that is moral, right or proper. That potential selfish choice may concern a political, financial or personal issue, and may even be something embarrassing to you or your company. But these are not "ethical" decisions. These situations call for knowing and doing what is right and having the courage to see it through all the way. How can something that is wrong be considered a right ethical decision?

As more healthcare professionals straddle the often conflicting demands between patient care, government regulatory mandates, health insurance requisites, legal directives, and administrative policies and procedures, it is well worth remembering that, while others may have a different "moral compass," there is only one true "North." Our compass needle should always point to the same direction. And in Medicine, the one constant compass point has always been, "First, do no harm."

Notes

Leadership Lessons From History
Part 25

Title: "Dead Horses"

No matter who originated this piece[*], all physician leaders should copy and paste this lesson to their wall.

The tribal wisdom of the Dakota Indians says that when you discover that you are riding a dead horse, the best strategy is to dismount. But in modern times, because heavy investment factors are taken into consideration, other strategies often are tried first by leaders, including the following:

- Buying a stronger whip.
- Changing riders.
- Threatening the horse with termination.
- Appointing a committee to study the horse.
- Arranging to visit other sites to see how they ride dead horses.
- Lowering the standards so that dead horses can be included.
- Reclassifying the dead horse as "living-impaired."
- Hiring outside contractors to ride the dead horse.
- Harnessing several dead horses together to increase speed.
- Providing additional funding and or training to increase the horse's performance.
- Doing a productivity study to see if lighter riders would improve the dead horse's performance.
- Declaring that the dead horse carries lower overhead and therefore contributes more to the bottom line than some other horses.

---

[*] One Internet source cited *The Dead Horse Strategies* as coming from the book, *Strategic Navigation*, by Bill Dettmer. Appendix F, pages 287-288; ASQ Press (2003).

- Rewriting the expected performance requirements for all horses.
- Do "creative accounting" by coding non-feed items to feed so that a budget variance does not have to be written.
- Promoting the dead horse.

If you do not believe the equivalent of the above happens in modern operational practices, then consider the last recorded words by General George A. Custer, at the Battle of Little Bighorn, when he ordered his outnumbered cavalry regiment to attack the combined Dakota-Sioux and Cheyenne Indian village of over 3,000 warriors, led by their famous native chiefs Crazy Horse and Sitting Bull. On first spying the immense Indian village, the General reportedly said: "Hurrah boys. We've got them!"

Leadership Lessons From History
Part 26

Title: "Leadership & Motivation"

Physician leaders can use this example to help them find the proper people motivation for difficult projects.

On the cold winter night of December 25-26, 1776, George Washington led his rag-tag army of just over two thousand men across the icy Delaware River to stage a surprise attack against the British mercenary Hessian defenders stationed in Trenton, New Jersey. That battle, and the subsequent victory at Princeton, turned the tide of the Revolutionary War in favor of the Colonist. No historian ever recorded the speech Washington must have made to his assembled troops on that Christmas night, before starting this arduous and dangerous journey, but I imagine it went something like this:

"Men, I've got news for you." George Washington said to his troops. "We're going to leave our warm cabins, tents and beds in the middle of this stormy night and cross a deep and quick running river, full of ice, in leaking barges that are likely to capsize and drown everyone. Then, in the snow, sleet and freezing rain, we're going to march nine miles to Trenton, in the dark, on slippery roads, where we will attack an entrenched military garrison that's the best trained soldiers in the world." At that moment, a soldier in the assembly raised his hand and said: "Excuse me General, but can you give us just one good reason why we should do all of this tonight, and in such bad weather, especially since our enlistments are almost up?" Stretching his head and torso high enough for everyone to see him, Washington replied: "Because the New Year is coming and I have been told by our spies that the Trenton Inn has just received a fresh supply of beer on tap!"

Although the above rendition is fictitious, James M. McPherson[*], the award-winning American Civil War historian, did write that President Abraham Lincoln once said, in a 1861 speech before the New Jersey legislature at the start of the war between the states, that something more motivating than just the notion of "fighting for National Independence" must have driven the men in Washington's army to persevere on that cold night, despite the poor odds and the even worse winter weather conditions they encountered. But, what that motivation was, Lincoln did not know. Obviously, Washington did find something to tell his men that worked. This is a sign of a great leader; every leader needs to find that successful motivation for others, especially in times of crisis. As to the story, after the fight, some of Washington's soldiers did break into the tavern and poured themselves a few drinks!

---

[*] James M. McPherson. Tried By War: Abraham Lincoln as Commander in Chief. The Pinguin Press, © 2008; Introduction; pp. 1-2. Paperback edition.

Notes

Leadership Lessons From History

Part 27

Title: "Sources of Inspiration"

As the following story illustrates, the next best idea in Medicine may come from outside the field. Physician leaders can do well to familiarize themselves with developments other than in their own specialty and adopt or borrow whatever is suitable for their particular situation.

Most people are familiar with the history of Henry Ford and the development of the car assembly line, which transformed the automotive industry in the United States. However, according to the AuSable-Oscoda Historical Museum (114 E. River Road, P.O. Box 679, Oscoda, Michigan 48750), years prior, Henry Ford had paid a visit to Oscoda and may have found his inspiration from a local dairy farm operated by a German-descent resident.

In 1911, the AuSable River was dammed and a hydro-electric plant was built that supplied power all the way to Flint, Michigan, which was a 100 miles away. A local business man, Mr. Carl E. Schmidt (1857-1934), ran the Serradella Farm using that new energy supply; originally, he had run a tannery in Detroit. Hearing of how efficiently he operated the farm, Henry Ford paid a visit and then went back and built his assembly line, substituting the process of milking cows for building cars. Further local ties to Henry Ford exist in that the area's sand originally was used to make his cars' first windshields.

The point is that often we do not need to re-invent the wheel, merely adopt it from another source. At one point, the University of Chicago required all of its professors - no matter how many Nobel Prizes they might have won - to attend classes outside of their own specialty area that were taught by fellow educators. New ideas for innovative medical programs may indeed owe their inspiration to such outside sources. After all, in this day and age, and to paraphrase an old saying, physician leaders really do need to innovate or perish!

Leadership Lessons From History
Part 28

Title: "Loss of Vision"

One characteristic of all great leaders is the ability to create a vision for others in the organization to follow. In creating the vision, physician leaders need to be vigilant that the vision is maintained down the chain of command without degradation. The following story shows how some middle managers lost sight of that vision in their drive for optimal manufacturing efficiency.

Henry Ford's unspoken social contract with his automotive assembly line workers was very simple: in exchange for relinquishing the prevailing individual craftsman ideology and method of building cars, he would have them perform the same, repetitive assembly line work all day long, but pay them the equivalent of twice the current average weekly wage. Unfortunately, that social contract of respecting (with higher pay) the workers' physical working condition was broken by his middle managers.

Near the City of Detroit is the Henry Ford House Museum. It is well worth a tourist visit. Inside a cottage house, next to the manor, is a floor display detailing the early history of the automotive assembly line. In one section, it stated that supervisors would terminate any worker on the spot if he left his post during their 10-hour-long shift, even for a single bathroom break! "There were plenty of other people willing to work under those conditions for that extra pay," management reasoned.

Overly strict company policies, such as the one above, not only can contribute to a lowering of employee morale, but also may backfire in promoting anti-management sentiment among the workers.

The essence of this article is this: unless your organization practices the "Golden Rule," the company's vision statement will be compromised and your people will become disengaged.

Leadership Lessons From History
Part 29

Title: "Life is About Pacing Yourself; Don't Run it as a Series of 100-Yard Dashes!"

Both at home and work, physician leaders need to learn how to pace themselves and their people. Often, their constant drive, competitive spirit, and high expectations result in physicians not only burning themselves out, but also the people around them. After all, fatigue is the twin sibling of failure. Additionally, there is a tendency in management to apply a manufacturing attitude toward organizational projects that require high human input or effort: i.e., many managers believe that fifty-percent of a project should be completed in fifty-percent of the assigned timeline. This could cause them to underestimate the potential of many good employees, just like the Seabiscuit story below.

Seabiscuit, the famous racehorse of the 1930s, was a pace stalker; a horse that would run from the middle of the pack, and then pull ahead at the end. Nonetheless, he lost the first 16 races because he was forced to keep up with the front-runners. But, in 1937, he won 11 of the 15 races he entered. On November 1, 1938, Seabiscuit beat another famous racehorse, War Admiral, in the "Match of the Century," a race listened to by 40 million people over the radio. For this feat, he was named, "American horse of the year" in 1938. When Seabiscuit retired in 1940, he was horse racing's all-time leading money winner.

Not everyone is a pace-setter (someone who races up front), nor should every situation or current condition be run from the front, or judged by his or her position at the middle of the race, or raced as if life were a series of high-energy, prematurely exhausting, 100-yard races. The mistake the initial owner made was not realizing Seabiscuit's true potential; a mistake the new owner's trainer rectified. The rest, as they say, is history!

Leadership Lessons From History
Part 30

Title: "Promoting Effective People"

Years ago, a psychological study confirmed something long suspected. During peacetime, the U.S. military preferentially promoted officers who looked the part: they were tall, handsome, and had a full set of hair. However, come wartime, and after the initial shake out period, the military promoted effective officers, even if they were short, fat, and bald! The same image bias exists in our political system. As per a 2009 article in TIME magazine, and as compared to the leaders in Europe and the rest of the world, Americans tend to elect charismatic business and political representatives who look the part.[*] There is no reason to believe that "beautiful people" also are not given preferential treatment in business organizations.

The point of the message is this: Does the equivalent of a "Cyrano de Bergerac" person exist inside your organization? Someone who is smart, talented, effective, and hard-working, but who suffers, just like the character in the play and movie, from an inferiority complex because he/she does not "look" the part? And so, he/she works behind the scenes while another person, who is more handsome and presentable from an image and publicity standpoint, takes the credit?

Who should you promote? What steps have you taken to ensure that truly effective people are recognized and promoted inside your organization? Long ago, symphony halls across the nation started holding "blind" orchestra auditions. Prospective musicians are being interviewed from behind a curtain where the judges cannot see them, only listen to them play. In the end, it is about the musical experience, not the looks. Similarly, for physicians, isn't it about the "Art of Medicine."

---

[*] Elliott, Michael. *No Charisma? Don't Worry, You Can Still Be a Leader.* Time Magazine; Monday, July 20, 2009. Retrieved from: http://www.time.com/time/magazine/article/0,9171,1909616,00.html#ixzz2Ccc2Qt9W

Leadership Lessons From History

Part 31

Title: "Updates & the HMS Hood, and the Sinking of the Bismarck"

May 27th is the anniversary of the sinking of the *Bismarck*, the great German battleship of WWII. Within its story is a lesson on the timely updating of existing equipment for all physician leaders to learn.

Commissioned originally in 1920, the noted British battleship *HMS Hood*, underwent a series of updates and improvements throughout the years so that, by 1940, it still was one of the few major ships England had that could match the great German battleship *Bismarck*. However, it did have one nagging and unaddressed design flaw brought on by newer weaponry technology: it was very susceptible to plunging shells from enemy vessels penetrating its upper deck.

Hence, when WWII broke out, the British Admiralty faced a difficult decision: if they updated the *Hood* now, it would leave a vital gap in their sea defenses, as the ship would have to be taken out of service. They decided to postpone the changes.

Years later, in May 1941, the German battleship, *Bismarck*, did indeed try to outrun the British blockade and the *HMS Hood* and another capital ship, the *Prince of Wales*, were sent to intercept and destroy this German threat to England's vital North Sea shipping. In a sea battle near Iceland, a lucky shell from the *Bismarck* found *Hood's* vulnerable spot and the entire 860-foot-long pride of the British fleet exploded massively. All but three of the *Hood's* 1421 seamen were lost at sea.

In retrospect, the *Hood* should have been updated BEFORE the war broke out. And that is the problem. Often, needed repairs are put off until there is a crisis. Whether or not it is aging medical hospital or office equipment, or old generation computers and EHRs, or updated coding programs, or tattered exam room tables and furniture, as operational budgets come under added pressures to scrimp and save, the natural tendency among healthcare administrators will be to continually postpone needed improvements, or transfer the assigned and budgeted funds to other areas — excusing such actions by characterizing all such updates as merely cosmetic changes, without any immediate return on investment value. Updates also reduce company quarterly profits and bureaucrats' bonuses. Unfortunately, many of those administrators who would make such decisions likely are not going to be there when it all blows up. Some may even know it. But, just like the captain of the *HMS Hood,* physician leaders certainly going to be at the center of the maelstrom when it does explode!

Leadership Lessons From History
Part 32

Title: "Saying No!"

There is a skill that all physician leaders need to cultivate if they are going to be successful: it is the ability to say, "No!" The following story illustrates what can happen when the one true expert on the subject defers to group-think.

On January 28, 1986, the American Space Shuttle Challenger blew up after takeoff. This tragedy was caused by freezing temperatures compromising the O-rings in the shuttle's solid rocket boosters (SBRs). Morton Thiokol was the contractor for the SRBs and, on the evening of January 27, a teleconference was held between Thiokol and the NASA launch people; NASA told them they were impatient for a go-launch recommendation. In making their final decision "to go ahead," Thiokol managers pressured their main engineer to suppress his concerns by – paraphrasing – telling him, "For once in your life, think like a manager not like an engineer!"

So ingrained are physicians to wishing to be of service and to fit in, that he/she could end up compromising their beliefs and efforts. This is where there is a need to break apart and assert your true value to the group or to the meeting: that of someone not only with medical training, but also someone who has dealt directly with patients and their real-world problems.

In these potentially confrontational situations, it often helps to reframe the question at hand. Using the above example to illustrate the point, instead of asking dissenters for "proof" that it was unsafe for the Challenger to fly, the question the group really should have asked was, "What evidence do we have that it is it safe to go!"

Leadership Lessons From History
Part 33

Title: "Administrative Think!"

Physicians new to a leadership position within a large organization are in for a shock. They will encounter a phenomenon I call, "Administrative Think." It is a completely different way for people to think and to view the world around them. Let me use the example below to illustrate the point.

A sheep herder was tending his flock one day at his farm when a man in a business suit stopped his car on the side road to the property and got out. Approaching the herder, the stranger asked if he could buy one of his 124 sheep. "That's amazing! One look and you knew exactly how many I have. Give me $50 and you can take one," said the farmer. The businessman handed over the money, picked up an animal, and started to walk to his car. "Hold on it, Mr. Administrator," said the farmer. Stopping, the stranger turned to the farmer and asked, "How did you know I was an administrator?" The herder took a deep breath in and said: **"Put my sheep dog down and I'll tell you!"**

In Plato's "Dialogues," the philosopher wrote about how some people viewed things not by direct observation, but through the shadows projected on a cave's walls by the light of the camp fire; they believed that the shadows, instead, were the "reality." And so is it with some administrators. They've worked alone in their office cave for so long that they've come to believe that the only reality is the endless stream of charts, tables, and reports at their desk. Not long ago, during the start of the economic downturn, several failed businesses took their federal bailout money and used it to give financial bonuses to their executives, prompting a public outcry. If those managers and executives truly deserved and had earned their bonuses, by meeting their productivity quotas and/or personal performance incentives, then why did the company go under in the first place?

In ending, the story of the Costa Concordia disaster comes to mind. Part for the reason for the chaos on board the sinking cruise ship during the accident, which left 17 dead and 15 unaccounted for, was due to the fact that **the passenger safety briefing had been scheduled THE NEXT DAY!** Administrative policies allowed the boat to sail first and hold the safety briefings <u>later.</u> This is "administrative think" at its finest!

Leadership Lessons From History
Part 34

Title: "The Need for a Devil's Advocate"

"Japan never declares war before attacking." And so stated Colonel Billy Mitchell back in 1932. Colonel Mitchell was an early pioneering aviation expert and enthusiast who challenged the current military leadership by proposing an expanded role for an independent Air Force, and for the inevitability of mass aerial warfare. He also challenged the prevailing land army suppliers, and the Navy's big-battleship financial interests of this country, by threatening their lucrative military contracts. Mitchell even demonstrated in 1921, to the amazement of all his critics, the ease at which just a few planes could sink the one of the world's most heavily armored battleships of the day, the WWI captured German ship *Ostfriesland*. He then proved to the embarrassed generals and admirals just how difficult it was to shoot down a fast flying plane by ground fire. They and the War Department responded to his visionary pronouncements by first demoting him, then removing him from active military service via a rigged court-martial trial. Billy Mitchell died a broken man in 1932. But before he died, and years before our national disaster on December 7th, 1941, a "day that will stand in infamy," Billy Mitchell predicted that Japan would initiate war with the United States with a surprise aerial attack on Pearl Harbor!*

Even to this day, too many organizations value and actively seek out and promote uniformity of agreement in its people, and avoidance of any open conflicts among its participants, sometimes even before the meeting begins! Dissenting members (playing *The Devil's Advocate* role) often are viewed with alarm and as threats to the cohesiveness of the group; they and their opposing views are considered obstructionist to leadership efforts at moving things along at a predetermined course of action. Much care is given to choosing the "right" members to seat at the table, people

---

* From the book *Flyboys*, 2003, Chapter Four; by James Bradley author of *Flags of Out Father*.

chosen mainly for their willingness to go along and not make waves, just like the former boardroom members at Enron. Unfortunately, being encumbered by same group-think, this type of company inbreeding and lack of leadership diversity limits an organization's ability to respond well to change, and to new challenges and threats. It is a sad fact that, in many organizations, and for people like Billy Mitchell, politics and bureaucracy often triumph over insightful visionary leadership.

Photo of display taken at the Wurtsmith Air Museum, Oscoda, Michigan. (See wurtsmithairmuseum.org.)

Notes

Leadership Lessons From History
Part 35

Title: "Being a Leader Means Being Prepared"

United States went to war with Germany three times and beat them every time, four times if you count General Washington's army crossing the Delaware in 1776 to fight the Hessians guarding Trenton, New Jersey. Everyone knows about WWI and WWII, but did you know there was a war between Germany and the U.S. that no one ever heard about?

In 1906, Argentina defaulted on a national loan to Germany. In defiance of the Monroe Doctrine, Germany's leader, Kaiser Wilhelm, sent a fleet of ships to invade the South American country and to take over its possessions and resources. Keeping track of the situation, President Theodore Roosevelt took immediate action and, without consulting Congress, maneuvered a U.S. navy flotilla to block the Germans. Even though at the time the German navy in total was three time the size of the U.S. sea forces, Theodore had sent more ships than Germany! The Kaiser backed down and the war was won without a single shot being fired.

Physician leaders need to be prepared; they need to develop a knack for anticipating events and of preparing for action should the threat or situation materialize. Just because every conceivable threat cannot be acted upon, this should not prevent a leader from using his/her judgment on focusing on the most probable, or on acting on those events now unfolding. It then becomes incumbent upon the leader to have the courage and fortitude to act before others are certain, or absolute proof is reached. As any beach surfer can tell you, one needs to be positioned ahead of the coming wave in order to ride it best. Trying to catch an ocean wave from behind is almost impossible.

Example: How many medical organizations were caught unprepared for the 2014 Ebola scare in this country? How many of these were warned, but disregarded the threat? How many failed to order in time the necessary personal protective equipment (PPE) for their medical personnel? During the severe acute respiratory syndrome (SARS) scare in 2003, medical masks became scarce world-wide; some were being sold for $50 each. How many healthcare administrators failed to learn from that example?

Leadership Lessons From History
Part 36

Title: "Whistle-Blowing"

At some point in their careers, physician leaders will need to deal with the issue of whistle-blowing, either individually or by one of their associates/employees. No topic is more mine-laden with personal and professional dangers, or more emotionally gut-wrenching. Few if any other issue causes as much ethical soul searching. And there are no good answers.

Currently, the world is facing a potentially serious threat from MERS, the Middle East Respiratory Syndrome from a new Coronavirus stain, which is similar to SARS virus that caused the world-wide outbreak in 2003. Dr. Ali Mohamed Zaki, discovered the deadly MERS virus in June, 2012, at a private hospital in the Middle East. Initially, he notified the local health ministry. He even sent them viral samples. But, upon not hearing back from them, he acted as a good global citizen and posted a warning on an international website that had been developed especially for this situation after the SARS incident in 2003. The health ministry was not pleased. As a reward for his good work, not only was Dr. Zaki forced to leave the hospital, but he also was deported from the country.

Recently, in South Africa, the provincial health authorities filed charges against three doctors who allegedly spoke out about the poor state of hospital infrastructure in the province. In 2009, two nurses, who anonymously had reported a delinquent doctor to the Texas Medical Board (TMB) over the quality of his patient care, faced retaliation by that doctor and their hospital administrator, who, nonetheless, had discovered the identities of the accusers. The nurses were fired from the county hospital and a county lawyer and sheriff cooperated in filing formal criminal charges against them; one nurse even had to face a court trial for her efforts to protect patients. Since then, the nurses have been vindicated. But in response, a state law was passed forbidding the Texas

Medical Board from accepting, and therefore acting upon, anonymous reports on physician complaints.

What To Do?

Even Superman, the mighty comic-book hero, needed a secret identity to protect him and those around him from his enemies. Is it any surprise then that ordinary men and women would seek similar anonymous protection before acting as whistle-blowers? Not many people know that Sherron Watkins, the former Enron vice-president and whistle-blower, initially posted her corporate financial accounting concerns anonymously in a memo to Chairman Ken Lay. It was only after he urged the sender to reveal his/her identity did she relent. Mr. Lay then had an "independent" law firm look into her allegations; no significant problems were "found." Little did Sherron know that the whole process was rigged; that all the bosses were in on the fix. And that is the problem. From Enron to the Watergate scandal, any potential whistle-blower is faced with the need to know, before acting, just how far up and down the dishonesty goes and the identity of all the perpetrators, accomplishers and collaborators in and outside the organization. They also have to contend with potentially corrupted political, enforcement or judicial systems.

There are no satisfactory answers to this dilemma. Whistle-blowers almost always face a catch-22 situation: if they go through regular channels and follow corporate procedures, they risk tipping off others and getting themselves into trouble. If they circumvent the system and are successful, they face prosecution for not following existing company protocols, rules or laws. The only really successful whistle-blower person I know was Washington Post's reporters Woodward and Bernstein's famous Watergate informer. Passing laws is not enough. Meanwhile, in England ...

> "An alleged cover-up of the health watchdog's failure to investigate a series of baby deaths reached to the highest ranks of the organization, it has been revealed."

Sources

(1) **Middle East coronavirus: No reward for man behind discovery.** http://gulfnews.com/opinions/columnists/middle-east-coronavirus-no-reward-for-man-behind-discovery-1.1194365

(2) **Whistleblowing doctors in trouble.** 2012-07-02 22:36. http://www.news24.com/SouthAfrica/News/Whistleblowing-doctors-in-trouble-20120702

(3) **Texas Physician Pleads Guilty in Whistle-Blowing Nurses Case. By** Robert Lowes. Medscape Medical News; November 7, 2011.

(4) FROM ENRON TO WORLDCOM AND BEYOND: LIFE AND CRIME AFTER SARBANES-OXLEY†

By KATHLEEN F BRICKEY. Washington University Quarterly. 2003. Vol. 81; 357-401.

(5) **Former chief of healthcare watchdog linked to 'cover-up' 6/20/13**

http://www.yorkshirepost.co.uk/news/main-topics/general-news/former-chief-of-healthcare-watchdog-linked-to-cover-up-1-5786650

Leadership Lessons From History
Part 37

Title: "I like bats much better than bureaucrats"

So stated past Oxford and Cambridge theologian and noted author, **C.S. Lewis** (November 29, 1898 – November 22, 1963). C. S. Lewis was the author of *The Chronicles of Narnia;* he also was a good friend and confidant of J. R. R. Tolkien, the author of *The Hobbit* and *The Lord of the Rings.* Lewis hated living in the Managerial Age. He equated Hell to the bureaucracy of the business concern, or of the government, where the greatest evils in the world were being committed "… in clean, carpeted and well-lighted offices by quiet men with white collars and cut fingernails."

American physicians have encountered the same "bureaucratic think" in their day-to-day dealings with governmental rules and regulations, the insurers' policies, and the never-ending adoption of prior-authorization policies, from everything from radiological procedures to drugs, to medical durable equipment.

Often, and in their quest to financially justify on paper their value to their contracted healthcare insurer, company, or governmental office, via the total dollars they saved, prior authorization units and their manages, operating in their own health care silos, pay little attention to how their policies and processes actually INCREASE the total health care costs. When the doctors' and patients' time, trouble, additional travel costs – gas at one point was over $4.00 a gallon – and all the financial consequences (e.g., lost time from work, etc.), and unintended ill-health effects, are included and their indirect and direct costs are added up, from the subsequent delays in diagnosis, treatment, or drug therapy, little true savings are likely to be achieved. At their core, many prior authorization and drug management programs simply cost-shift an expense to others, or use stalling tactics to delay and frustrate requested health care expenditures, medically necessary or not.

Which leads to this request: before implementing a prior authorization program, including any clinical patient reports and evaluations, the bureaucrats need to do an impact study on the total additional health care costs that will be incurred downstream by all the stakeholders. Only those programs that achieve health care savings for the whole system should be implemented. Additionally, there needs to be a rule forbidding government or insurance forms with microscopic letters. In order to save on paper costs, many are squeezing as much as they can onto every page. Ever try to read and fill out a question sheet page full of 8-font type?

Notes

Leadership Lessons From History
Part 38

Title: "Making Operational Music Together"

The highly acclaimed musical conductor of the Los Angeles Philharmonic, Gustavo Dudamel, once was quoted as saying, "An orchestra is a model for an ideal global society—a symbol. You have to create harmony. Everyone has to listen to each other, ...this large, complex group of people with different personalities has to communicate. You (also) have to have discipline (and high standards)." Physician leaders looking to improve overall quality and efficiency in their workplace would do well to heed this advice as it is the underlying basis of W. Edwards Deming pioneering work and teachings on manufacturing efficiency and constant quality improvement.

William Edwards Deming was born in Sioux City, Iowa, on 14 October 1900 to William Albert Deming and Pluma Irene Edwards. His mother, Pluma, had studied in San Francisco and was a musician. So it should come of no surprise to learn that, besides having graduate degrees in mathematics and mathematical physics, Deming also studied music theory and played several instruments; he even composed two masses, several canticles as well as an easily sung version of the **Star Spangled Banner**.

The point of the lesson is this: In reading through Deming's 14 Quality Points, think of yourself as the "maestro" of a complex orchestra about to play and perform a new musical piece for the first time. How many similarities are there? Receiving constant feedback and actively listening to each another are vital qualities to an organization. What about opportunities for employees to train? To practice? To learn? How important it is for the leader to keep a constant pulse on the whole?

Deming's 14 Quality Points:

- Create constancy of purpose for improvement of product or service
- Adopt a new philosophy
- Do not depend on mass inspection for quality control
- Stop awarding business on the basis of price tag
- Improve quality, costs will decrease because of fewer reworks, etc
- Institute more thorough, better job-related training
- Institute leadership
- Drive out fear
- Break down barriers
- Eliminate slogans, exhortations, and targets
- Eliminate work standards
- Remove the barriers that rob employees of their right to pride of workmanship
- Institute a vigorous program of education and self-improvement
- Put everybody to work to accomplish the transformation

Sources:

(1) **Bravo, Gustavo! How Maestro Dudamel Is Saving Classical Music Feb 6, 2012 12:00 AM EST**

http://www.thedailybeast.com/newsweek/2012/02/05/bravo-gustavo-how-maestro-dudamel-is-saving-classical-music.html

(2) **Deming's 14 Quality Points**

http://www.beowulf.org/pipermail/beowulf/1998-October/001824.html

Notes

Photo of display taken at the Wurtsmith Air Museum, Oscoda, Michigan. (See wurtsmithairmuseum.org.)

Leadership Lessons From History
Part 39

Title: "High Flying Performers"

This is one of my favorite stories. The original Flying Tigers were a dedicated and talented cadre of Pre-Pearl Harbor attack, WWII volunteer American airplane pilots who flew second-hand, single wing fighter planes as mercenaries for the Chinese Air Force against their Japanese invaders. Under the visionary and exceptional leadership skills of their commanding officer, Claire L. Chennault, they developed and implemented a successful strategy of combining an early air-raid warning system with a "climb high, then dive down and attack" approach to shoot down nearly 300 enemy planes with the loss of only 14 of their own in just 18 months. And this was done during a time when the Japanese "Zero" fighter plane otherwise ruled the skies!

The lesson for all physician leaders is this: Although acquiring the latest and greatest equipment is nice and helpful, outcome success more often than not is determined by a small group of motivated, well-trained, and disciplined employees; by fellow doctors and providers taking advantage of their current strengths to accomplish much, especially when directed by leaders who not only think outside the box, but also are willing to buck the conventional thinking and practices of others. Enlisting the confidence, support and help of the local population (i.e., customers, patients and communities) at hand also is supremely beneficial.

Get them Tigers!

Photo of display taken at the Wurtsmith Air Museum, Oscoda, Michigan. (See wurtsmithairmuseum.org.)

Leadership Lessons From History
Part 40

Title: "Supply Lines"

This story is a continuation of the last; it is a book-end to the previous piece on the success of the "Flying Tigers" of WWII.

The adventurer, Merian C. Cooper, is best remembered at the director and producer of the classic 1933 monster movie, King Kong. But his other achievements include being a WWI American aviator, a volunteer aviator for the Polish government in their dispute with the Soviets, an organizer and leader of big game safari expeditions, and a silent film photographer of the wonders of the world. His movie credits also include the development of the big screen film format popular in the 1950s and 1960s.

But what has been forgotten was that, in WWII, Merian C. Cooper was a logistic officer for Jimmie Doolittle's bomber raid on Tokyo, and then the chief of staff for Claire L. Chennault's Flying Tigers. In fact, he was the originator of the "Burma Hump," the dangerous flying supply route over the Himalayas that kept the whole operation going.

The lesson for physician leaders is this: you are only as good as your supply officer allows you to be. Cooper's exceptional organizational skills kept dangerous safaris in the field, world-exploring movie junkets traveling, and big Hollywood movie productions going. These skills were put to good use in the Pacific for the U.S. Army Air Force in WWII. In recognition of his military service and contributions to our nation, he was given the high honor of being one of the few officers on board the U.S.S. Missouri when the Japanese signed the peace treaty.

Leadership Lessons From History
Part 41

Title: "Future Anticipation"

Things seldom stay the same. The architects of New York City's Twin Towers found that out the hard way. When they designed their buildings, in the 1970s, they anticipated a possible and accidental mid air airplane collision and designed them to withstand such an impact. After all, in the 1940s, in a fog, a medium bomber had flown into the Empire State Building. However, they neglected to think ahead. Despite all the aviation experience of the last sixty years, where commercial plane sizes steadily increased in each succeeding decade, <u>the Twin Towers' were built to withstand a collision with a current jet airplane, not a future one</u>, even though the buildings' operational lifetime was expected to be over fifty years. The added jet fuel carried in the larger commercial planes of 2001 generated much higher temperatures, when the planes exploded, than the buildings' designs were intended to withstand, and the extra heat ended up melting the floors' supports, resulting in a pancake effect, which toppled the towers.

The lesson for all physician leaders is this: whether or not it is operational or information technology issues, it pays to consider the future. The computer Y2K crisis, at the turn of the 21st century, is a good lesson on the failure to think ahead. Yet another example: Years ago, CPT codes were only 4 digits long. When 5-digit CPT codes were introduced, many healthcare companies were caught off guard as their legacy systems limited them to only entering four digits. Which is a valuable lesson: in developing your organization's policies and procedures, think ahead and try not to box yourself in should events change!

Antoine-Jean Gros (French, 1771-1835), *Napoleon on the Battlefield of Eylau*, 1807, oil on canvas, 41 1/4 x 57 1/8 in. (104.9 x 145.1 cm), Toledo Museum of Art (Toledo, Ohio), Purchased with funds from the Libbey Endowment, Gift of Edward Drummond Libbey, 1988.54 Photo Credit: Photography Incorporated, Toledo

Leadership Lessons From History
Part 42

Title: "Medical Providers are Being Stress Fractured"

In June, 1812, Napoleon invaded Russia along with an army of 600,000 men; fewer than 100,000 made it back. During their ignoble military withdraw, in the middle of a terrible winter, thousands of soldiers died of exposure to the intense cold. However, along the retreat route, in the little Lithuanian town of Vilnious, modern grave site forensic analysis of the soldier's bones revealed an interesting fact: many of the soldiers had suffered from stress (marching) fractures of their feet.

Because the journey into Russia would be so far, Napoleon and his officers meticulously planned every aspect of the invasion force, including detailing all the equipment each soldier would have to carry in order to accomplish their military mission. Each piece was confirmed as necessary. Each article was deemed vital to their overall success. Nonetheless, this meant that each man had to carry over 70 lbs of equipment on his back. It was too much. Literally, their leaders broke their soldier's feet!

As the delivery of quality healthcare continues to move forward in this nation, whether or not it be through patient centered medical homes or accountable care organizations, and as our governmental and healthcare insurance leaders continue to issue collective proclamations and increasing documentation requirements, regarding never-ending demands on the primary care providers' time, the summation of all these efforts is rapidly approaching the point of fracturing the very bones of the providers on the front lines of medical care in this nation.

Peripheral items, such as demonstrating, in detail, meaningful EHR use, or perpetually dealing with subcontracted radiological and pharmacy management companies and their constant faxes for prior authorization information, or their rotating substitutions for alternative prescribed drugs, and the patient paperwork involving durable medical equipment re-authorization — in effect, questioning and changing every medical decision made — are now so intrusive as to demand an ever increasing amount of the doctor's time away from direct patient care; doctors are spending just as much time (or even more!) filling out the paper and computer work involved in the office visit as in taking to the patient.

And this is just part of it. According to a 2009 analysis quoted by Medical Economics, in order to fulfill all the preventive care and chronic disease management guidelines, a typical primary care doctor would have to work 22 hours a day!* Is it any wonder that more physicians than ever are suffering from symptoms of burn-out?

As it was in the past, there's no doubt that, in the minds of Napoleon and his generals, each piece of equipment they asked their soldiers to carry on their journey into Russia was important and necessary. Their mistake was they forgot they were leading an army of men not mules! Unfortunately, History seems to be repeating itself, this time in patient care. Now is our "winter of our discontent."

---

* Study quoted from: Charlotte Huff. *4 Ethical dilemmas facing physicians*. August 7, 2014. http://medicaleconomics.modernmedicine.com

Notes

Leadership Lessons From History
Part 43

Title: "Leaders Need Champions"

All physician leaders need champions, one or more persons of influence inside and out their parent organization who not only will promote their talents and skills, but also assist and defend them against professional and personal attacks and accusations. If General, then future U.S. President, Ulysses S. Grant had not the benefit of such support, we might not have heard of him in history.

Shortly after his victory at the Battle of Shiloh (April 1862), during the early stages of the American Civil War, and despite it being one of very few Union victories over the South at the time, General Grant suddenly found himself being accused of drunkenness and facing demands that he be relieved of his command. President Lincoln, himself, had to stop the rumor, by a strong show of support. Interesting enough, several months prior, after his capture of Fort Donelson in Tennessee, Grant had been stripped of his command by his jealous superior officer, General Halleck, **for not filing his military reports on time**! This was done with the consent of the top Union Army commander at the time, General MClellan. As it turned out, a lazy telegraph operator had stacked Grant's reports away and had failed to forward them to Headquarters. Grant appealed to his congressional sponsor, Elihu Washburne, who then personally spoke to Lincoln. Lincoln then asked for a full military inquiry into the matter, which settled the issue in favor of Grant; he soon was given his command back again.[*]

The point of this lesson is this: on their way to the top, physician leaders are going to have to fight some battles along the way. Unfortunately, some of those battles will be against people from within the organization, people who are jealous or envious of their success and who will actively

---

[*] James M McPherson. Tried by War: Abraham Lincoln as Commander in Chief. Penguin Book; © 2008.

or passively obstruct, or sabotage, his or her climb up the corporate ladder. During these trying times, it will help to have strong support from champions who will stand up with you against these accusers and spoilers. Otherwise, your career may end up being a footnote somewhere.

Leadership Lessons From History
Part 44

Title: "Keeping to One's Mission"

Whether or not you call it, "Keeping your eye on the ball," or "Begin with the end in mind," one thing all physician leaders need to do is to constantly remind themselves to keep to their "Mission." The following true story illustrates this point.

One night, during WWII, all the senior officers of a U.S. aircraft carrier were called to a meeting by the captain. At the meeting, the flight commander informed them of the critical situation: their planes and fliers would not return from its enemy bombing run until nightfall. As it was, landing on an aircraft carrier during daytime was dangerous enough; but to do it at night would require the ship not only to turn on all its lights, but also to hold to a steady course and speed during the aircrafts' landings. The captain then added that, as they were operating in enemy waters, this meant the ship and all the men on board would be in danger of being torpedoed and sunk by any submarine operating in the area. He then asked all the operational officers at the table for their recommendations.

It was unanimous. One by one, the operational officers said the same thing: the planes and the 100 men flying them would have to be sacrificed for the sake of the ship and the lives of the hundreds of men on board. Of course, they would try to save as many of the flyers they could after they crash-landed in the ocean, but doing so in the dark would be a near impossible task. Silently, the captain listened to his men. When they were done, he rose and said, "Without those planes and flyers, we're no not a fighting warship, but just a big, useless boat in the sea." He then gave the order to proceed with the landings. Fortunately, there were no enemy submarines nearby and all the planes and men flying them arrived safely on the aircraft carrier. It may not have been the safest decision, but it was the right one.

How many of us would have been as courageous as this captain? How many of us, when faced with constantly conflicting priorities and crucial decisions, are able to clearly focus on the prime mission of the organization, and how the choices, proposals or alternatives either do or do not support that mission? Thinking back to the past few years, can you think of a few leadership decisions that did not align with your organization's stated mission? Were these choices "right" decisions or "safer" one?

Leadership Lessons From History
Part 45

Title: "Expert Advice"

One skill all physician leaders need to learn is when to listen to "expert" advice, and when to go against the grain. The following stories demonstrate how industry experts can be wrong at times.

Frank Sinatra was known as a difficult actor to deal with. A perfectionist with his work, Sinatra believed in getting it right the first time, whether or not it was with his music or movie scenes; often, Sinatra would record his songs or finish his scenes just in one take. Sinatra caused additional problems while filming the classic WWII movie, *Von Ryan's Express*. Anxious to produce a sequel, the movie company's executives wanted Sinatra's character to survive. Nonetheless, having a better sense of the dramatic than the movie "experts," Sinatra stuck to his guns and insisted on Von Ryan dying in the end. Sinatra won out, and it became one of his best movie roles ever. More recently, following his huge success with *Star Wars*, George Lucas had to appeal to Paramount Pictures to agree to release his next project, *Raiders of the Lost Ark*, as the "experts" at his previous movie company had passed on the project!

Switching to the auto industry, going into the 21st century, I attended the Detroit Auto Show where a display floor representative from one of the major U.S. auto companies bragged how they had scuttled their corporate electric car experimental program. It seems their experts had determined such cars would never sell. Meanwhile, the risk-adverse upper management and bean-counting experts at another major U.S. auto company were planning to end the production of their classic sports car. Updating it would be too expensive. It was only through the determined efforts of a small group of dedicated car enthusiasts within the company, working invisibly behind the scenes on a new version of the car, that the famous auto brand was saved.

The reason for bringing up these examples is to point out a common fallacy: experience does not always equate to expertise. The movie executives may have been great at producing, budgeting and distributing movies, but they had no artistic or dramatic sense. The high auto executives lacked vision, imagination and a "passion" for cars. Not everything is measured in dollars and cents. In planning for and building his theme park in Orlando, Florida, Walt Disney had to overrule the objections of all his managers! So, before following "expert," advice, ask yourself this question: "Is the issue playing into their strengths or their weaknesses?"

Notes

Leadership Lessons From History
Part 46

Title: 'Innovation'

Years ago my family and I paid a visit to Galena, Illinois, the home of Civil War General, Ulysses S. Grant. While there, I learned a valuable lesson that has escaped mention in tourist books. Nonetheless, it offers a timely reminder for all physician leaders of the importance of innovation.

Galena, Illinois, got its economic start from the nearby lead mining operations. However, at the time, as the Galena River was right off the Mississippi River, it also was a major hub for all the steamboat traffic going from St. Paul, Minnesota, all the way down to St. Louis. Understandably, many of Galena's main businessmen had strong economic ties to this water-based commerce. Hence, when the first railroads were being built in the Midwest, it was no surprise that Galena's leaders turned down a request to run a railroad through their town. At best, they saw no future in the proposal; at worse, it could turn out to be a possible competitor to their steamboat-based economy. Dismayed, the railroad company executives turned to their second choice to build their railroad hub – Chicago. The rest is history. Chicago flourished while Galena's economy floundered and then sank with demise of the steamboat era.

Simply put, Galena's leaders failed to understand their business: they thought they were in the steamboat business when, in fact, they were into TRANSPORTING goods – period! They did not consider the future. They missed getting in on the ground floor of the railroad boom in America. In the same vein, a 2013 Forbes article discusses the consequences of missing innovative trends and the applicability of those lessons to healthcare. CEO Steve Ballmer was ousted from Microsoft due to the company repeatedly missing out on new market segments to competitors, such as Google, the iPhone and the iPad. In part, this was due to Microsoft appointing old-thinking leaders to their new emerging business ventures and then underfunding them. As Forbes commentator David Chase* wrote, "...it's imperative that the innovators are free to unleash innovation critical to the enterprise's long-term survival." In short, does your organization shackle or encourage and financially support your innovators?

---

* David Chase. **Lessons for CEOs. Ballmer's Anomaly: Lesson For CEOs Who Don't Want To Get Ousted.** http://www.forbes.com/sites/davechase/2013/08/24/ballmers-anomaly-lesson-for-ceos-who-dont-want-to-get-ousted/?goback=.gde_1005057_member_268336062#!

Leadership Lessons From History
Part 47

Title: "Procession"

The "Five P's" of Operations Management include: People, Plant, Parts, Process, and Planning. To this set I have added my own unique component: Procession.

By the term, "Procession," I mean not only the passing of time or an era (e.g., the astronomical *Procession of the Equinoxes*), but also the passing on or succession of a job or a leadership position to another person, similar to a royal procession following the coronation of a new king or queen. That is to say, all physician leaders should anticipate and plan for not only the "here and now," but also incorporate into their planning an automatic anticipation of future changes in personnel, materials and circumstances.

A complete circle of the *Procession of the Equinoxes*, through each of the *Signs of the Zodiac*, takes more than 24,000 years. As the earth wobbles through one sign to another, the star, *Polaris*, does not always point "north." Unless today's leaders are aware of this change, they can easily lead tomorrow's organization astray by "hitching their wagon" to the wrong star!

Also, leaders frequently make the mistake of planning their operational processes based on the existing skill set or makeup of their current employees, forgetting that, over time, people may come and go, or even change. Years ago, an auto worker once told me that, whenever a particular man went on vacation, it threw their entire assembly line out of whack. This worker was nearly seven feet tall and easily could reach up and attach his assigned auto component in time; the same job required at least two men whenever he went on vacation, and, even then, the line needed to occasionally stop and wait for the two of them to finish installing the part!

Lastly, how many physician leaders have made plans for their own succession? How many have individualized their current operations and organizational chart or structure to suit only them and no one else? It's not unusual to find organizations that are left in an operational mess whenever key leaders leave or become ill. As *Alexander the Great* lay dying in his bed, his generals asked, "To whom will you leave your great empire to?" Reportedly, Alexander said, "To the strongest!" It was not the wisest of plans.

Leadership Lessons From History
Part 48

Title: "Cutbacks"

Every organization goes though times of growth and contraction. Physician leaders need to be adept at managing both time periods Rapid expansion, faster than they could control, track, and manage, doomed many HMOs during the managed care consolidation period in the 1990s and early 2000s. On the other hand, in the same time period, and anticipating a drastic drop in inpatient care, hospitals fired too many nurses, who then migrated to other forms of outpatient care. This left some hospitals so short of nursing staff that some facilities resorted to auctioning off, in ever increasing hourly wage levels, their unfilled nursing shifts until enough people volunteered for overtime duty. This gets me to my next point.

Abraham Lincoln loved to tell this story: There once was a farmer and his mule. Every day the farmer used his mule to plow the land. But, as the price of hay had increased, the miserly farmer continually, over time, decreased the amount of hay he was feeding the animal each day until he got the animal "accustomed" to not eating anything. Meanwhile, the mule continued to plow the same acres of land every day without let up. Then one morning, to the amazement and consternation of the farmer, he went to the barn and saw that the mule had the gall to go and die on him!

Unfortunately, even in healthcare, many administrators think like the above farmer. Anxious to have his divisional budget fit into a preconceived financial plan from top-down management, where pre-determined corporate profits held greater priority over any operational reality, a director repeatedly made his managers revise their medical employee staff and physician payroll budgets based on ever shorter historical trends. Unfortunately, patients do not always get sick on schedule, but are very much prone to ups and downturns. As might be expected, on the next quarter, the division severely exceeded those pre-projected expenses. The director "solved" his budget variance problem by deciding not to pay the physicians.

As unbelievable as the above may seem, the same happened recently in some South African hospitals that faced an acute shortage of doctors due to these professionals leaving their posts in protest. According to the Regional Chairperson of the South African Medical Association, the Eastern Cape Province failed to honor the doctors' contracts and regularly pay the physicians!*

---

* **Docs leave hospitals over pay.** Iafrica.com Fri, 06 Sep 2013. http://business.iafrica.com/news/878583.html

Leadership Lessons From History
Part 49

Title: "The Value of Serendipity"

In the winter months of 1775-1776, General George Washington and his American Continental Army for Independence had a problem. Although they had the British bottled up in Boston, they had no way to force them to leave. Then, an American privateer schooner, the *Lee*, under Captain John Manley, captured a British supply ship, the brig *Nancy*, just off the Boston shore. The enemy ship contained tons of war supplies, including cannon shots and mortars. While valuable, Washington could not make full use of the supplies until, one day in January, 25-year-old Henry Knox, a Boston bookseller, showed up with a surprise in toe. He had gone to Fort Ticonderoga, by Lake Champlain in upper New York, and, in the rain, sleet, snow, ice and freezing stormy weather, he and his men managed to drag 58 mortars and cannons 300 miles to Boston, not losing a single one of them along the way! Washington then positioned his new artillery pieces on the Dorchester Heights, which had a commanding view not only of the city of Boston, but also of all the British ships in the harbor, rendering both susceptible to their bombardment. After abandoning an unsuccessful attempt to take the heights by land assault, the British were forced to evacuate the city by sea in March of that year.[*]

Fortune favors the bold (Virgil, 70 BC to 19 BC). But what the quote does not say is how serendipity plays a role in making use of that good fortune when it arrives. How often do we come across something good but not useful right at that moment? Physician leaders need to develop that special inner "tingling" sense to know, without absolute proof or logic, when something is going to be needed in the future. As in the above example, the captured artillery supplies but without cannons were good, but not as useful until later; and the cannons that Knox delivered to Washington's army besieging the city of Boston would not have been

---

[*] McCullough, David. "1776." Simon & Schuster, New York, © 2006.

nearly as useful without the added cannonballs and mortar shots. It is the bringing of the two together, in synergistic fashion, which was instrumental in resolving the six-month long siege of Boston.

In our ever-changing world of healthcare, physician-leaders need to allow for unexpected "gifts" or surprises and have the resources available and waiting for the right opportunity. In the end, I imagine, Henry Knox got his Boston bookstore back, and in the process acquired at very grateful lifetime customer!

Leadership Lessons From History
Part 50

Title: "The Value of Non-Events"

Meaningful and reliable individual physician quality medical practice measurements are in a state of evolutionary development here in the United States by healthcare insurers, research-based educational institutions, interested third parties, and governmental agencies. Whether or not the data will lead to actual physician ratings available to the public on the Internet, remains to be seen. Already, Medicare financial physician payment information is being released. However, in the rush to develop and make available such complex information for consumers of healthcare services, there is the risk that pertinent physician (and other healthcare providers') measurements regarding the value of medical non-events will be left out of the quality equations. Without these objective comparative measurements, such disclosures run the risk of degenerating into mere social network commentary open to misinformation, bias and personal opinions.

What is a medical non-event? Simply put, it is any intervention, service or patient contact (direct or indirect) by an effective physician which, for the better, changes or improves the medical life of an individual. Think of the movie, "It's A Wonderful Life," and you will get the picture. What is the "value" of a timely cancer diagnosis by an alert physician of melanoma on the skin of a patient that results in early and successful removal before spreading? Or of a correct diagnosis made immediately in the emergency room, sparing the patient the ordeal of going through wasteful and unnecessary additional medical tests and services? What about an avoided heart attack or stroke because a physician encouraged a patient to stop smoking early in life? My guess is that these efforts are not appreciated, or counted! All too often, administrators substitute processing measures for outcome events; this is especially true for events that never happened.

In the classic ancient military strategy book, *The Art of War* by Sun Tzu, there is the story about a skilled physician who was asked by his lord if he were the greatest healer in all China. The physician replied that he was not. While his wide-spread fame and reputation was the result of performing successful surgeries, administering healing medicines and performing other therapeutics after his patients became sick, his brother was capable of healing people at the very first sign of their malady; hence, his brother's greatness as a physician is only known to the people in his village. But his oldest brother is even better. He is so great a physician that he is capable of healing people before they themselves know they are sick, and he does it without charge; hence, his patients often are not aware that they even have been cured. Yet, despite his brother's marvelous skill as a healer, only the members of his family know of his wonderful deeds.

All those involved in the process of medical provider measurements would do well to read the words of Sun Tzu.

Leadership Lessons From History
Part 51

Title: "The Captain of the Ship"

The captain of the ship is entitled to know the condition of his vehicle at all times. It's a simple ethical principle, and one that is often ignored, whether or not the "captain" is a physician leader or a president. It also applies to a patient when the "vehicle" is his or her own body.

At one point in the popular movie about the early days of America's Mercury Astronaut Program, *The Right Stuff*, the administrators back at Mission Control in Cape Canaveral were planning to withhold important information from the orbiting astronaut, John Glenn, regarding a flight hazard warning light. The blinking sensor indicated a possible malfunction in the heat shield apparatus of his vehicle. If it came loose during re-entry, the Mercury space capsule would burn up in the upper atmosphere. The administrators calculated that, as John Glenn could do nothing about it anyway, giving him the bad news would only cause him unnecessary worry. That's when another astronaut spoke up and reminded them that a captain of the ship has a right to know the condition of his vehicle at all times; and that they had better tell him or he will!

Unfortunately, years later, such a real life scenario was played out, this time with the space shuttle, Columbia. Back at mission control, the NASA's flight directors were informed that some of the booster rockets' insulation might have peeled off during lift-off and broken some of the insulating tiles on the spacecraft. And just like in the movie, the administrators concluded that informing the crew members would be pointless. They even turned down the opportunity to re-direct orbiting U.S. military satellites to take pictures in space of the scuttle, to inspect for damages, just in case.

The captain has a right to know the condition of his vehicle. Only in dire circumstances is it ethical for a doctor to withhold bad medical news from a patient. It is never right not to tell a leader bad news, even a U.S. president, about his "ship" or operating executive programs once problems are reasonably suspected or known. Yet, such paternalistic attitudes and self-serving behaviors happen all the time. Physician leaders clearly need to articulate this principle to their people — and never tolerate anyone breaking it, either by their people or by other leaders. The captain has a right to know the condition of his ship. It's that simple.

Leadership Lessons From History
Part 52

Title: "Middle Managers"

Sun Tzu's *The Art of War, Complete Text and Commentaries*, includes an admonition for leaders to be cognitive of middle managers.* This ancient Chinese warning has several levels of meaning. Middle managers will stick together. If left unchecked, they will proliferate until they paralyze an organization with bureaucratic red tape. In an effort to distinguish themselves from their counterparts, and be promoted, some middle managers will take unwarranted risks, authorize self-serving ventures, or implement policies that are contradictory to the company's stated values and mission. They even will compromise a company's end results if, in their own little silo of operations, it will benefit their area.

Ambitious middle managers have exceed their authority, even to the point of endangering other peoples' lives, authorized dehumanizing work policies, and cheated their employees out of their pay, by altering the number of hours they worked, firing any employee who complained. Greedy middle managers have put off necessary safety repairs, as the maintenance delay would lead to a loss of quarterly production, reducing their incentive pay. In a failing hospital, discharges and new admissions were held up, reducing patient turnover and overall profits, because the maintenance manager found it financially advantageous for his department to delay ordering wheelchair repair parts until the requisitions could be done in bulk. Two enterprising middle managers even once were caught manufacturing a crisis at work so that they could come in with solutions and be promoted!

However, there is another frustrating trait common to many middle managers; I call it "Situational Memory Amnesia." Let me explain. Once, I ordered wonton soup along with my a-la-cart dinner; my wife ordered

---

* Translated by Thomas Cleary. Shambhala Publications, Inc. Boston & London, 2003.

from the existing Chinese menu, which included a free cup of soup. But, when the dishes arrived, my wife was disappointed to see that her soup was not wonton, but egg-drop soup. Sensing her objection, I offered to switch dishes with her, which she eagerly accepted. After taking two sips of her broth, my wife said to me, "The wonton soup is really good today. You should have gotten this instead!"

Another example: a middle manager once promised me a certain office, but withdrew the offer when another doctor claimed seniority and took it instead. Two years later I was asked to move from my present office space because a new physician liked its proximity to the laboratory. When I declined, claiming my right to the office under the principal of seniority, that very same manager said, "But you don't understand. I already *promised* him your office!"

As Sun Tzu repeatedly pointed out, trustworthiness is an essential quality of leadership; instituting productive, efficient, and mutually cohesive operations management policies are others. Make sure your middle managers follow these principles. Self-serving lapses of memory should be discouraged.

Notes

Leadership Lessons From History
Part 53

Title: "Magic Acts"

Physician leaders need to avoid being fooled by magic acts.

We all have seen skillful magicians on television, stage, or even in a room or sidewalk, perform amazing tricks of dexterity and illusion. Everyone witnessing these fantastic acts will testify willingly, in any court of law, that they saw an entire elephant magically disappear in front of them, or that the magician teleported an assistant from one cabinet to another, even after sawing the lovely lady in half. We are constantly amazed how dealers can perform impossible card tricks. Some even can read our minds by picking out the very card we selected at random without his or her knowledge or input. The fact that neither you nor I can tell you how these tricks are performed, in no way prevents us from recognizing that they are tricks; that they are not real!

Nonetheless, leaders, groups, organizations, governments, and even courts are taken in repeatedly by skillful manipulators of data, words, and events. Just like world-class magicians, skillful lawyers are able to fool judges and juries. Just like card sharks, experienced politicians, administrators, bureaucrats, and even drug companies, can manipulate data to give it their desired, self-serving spin. By carefully choosing their words and presenting their questions in a predetermined and orchestrated manner, surveys can lead the "customer" into selecting the very opinions they want.

There are times when physician leaders need to listen to their instincts and not be fooled or manipulated by others, even if what they are saying appears logical at first sight. When Galileo first presented his controversial theory, that the sun was the center of our planetary system and not the Earth, the Catholic Church did everything it could to discredit the notion. Their supporters even proved mathematically that the Earth indeed was the center of the universe. It turns out that the earth-centric equation was equally "correct," but simpler.

My college advanced mathematics professor once proved to everyone in our class that, "one equaled zero." Only two students out of thirty challenged his finding. Years later, as a resident in the hospital, and applying Ockham's razor, a tool that has never failed me, I had to choose between two clinical theories: select people, belonging to a minority, were having their immune system exhausted by repeated infections with sexually transmitted diseases, or that a new, and yet medically undiscovered, virus was responsible for their skin cancers and respiratory infections. Guess which possibility was accepted by the medical experts? Guess which one I thought was right?

The mark of a great leader is the ability to distinguish between truth and the tricks performed by magicians. If the ancient pharaoh, Ramses, had listened to Moses and not to the priests of the temple and their floor act, turning their rods into snakes, he would have saved himself a pocketful of trouble!

Notes

Leadership Lessons From History
Part 54

Title: "Risk-Taking Leaders"

Some leaders are gamblers. You know who they are. Every organization, hospital, or provider group has at least one; someone whose yearly achievements and production are heads above everyone else. He or she is the darling of the organization, the up-and-coming new star. The shortcuts this leader takes never seem to amount to anything and everyone is on board with him/her because, by ripple effect, this person also makes them look good. If the leader is the head of a noticeable business concern, he/she may become even a media darling – an example for all to aspire to become. All until everything collapses!

During the Pacific War in World War II, the aggressive natured Admiral Halsey had his carrier task force abandon its protective coverage of the Allied Philippine invasion fleet at Leyte Gulf, and, instead, had his ships sail full speed ahead to intercept a group of Japanese warships that had been spotted to the north. It was a trap. Those Japanese ships were bait. Meanwhile, the real invasion intercepting Japanese fleet, including the biggest battleship in the world, was sailing toward Leyte Gulf from the South. Our fighting forces were in mortal danger of being completely destroyed on the beach. Left behind to defend our troops was a rag-tag collection of small carriers, old destroyers and destroyer escorts. With nothing to lose, they threw themselves at the Japanese fleet with reckless abandon. It was suicide. And many brave U.S. sailors and aviators lost their lives in that desperate sea fight.

In what can only be described as a miracle, the audacity of our fighting sailors manning those outgunned ships – in attacking the bigger Japanese fleet instead or retreating – so unnerved the Japanese that Admiral Kurita called off the attack. All our soldiers on that Philippine beach, and the sailors on the transport and supply ships, were saved.

When aggressive leaders guess wrong, or when their reckless actions have dire consequences for their fellow colleagues and/or institution, others usually have to step up and salvage the organization; and they are the ones that pay, in effort, time, and in money, for this leader's excesses. The media continually publishes stories of high-performing hospital groups, medical organizations, and even physicians and other providers, failing audits, resulting in thousands, if not millions, of dollars in recoveries. Wall Street is full of such financial sad stories.

Undoubtedly, there are gifted individuals who rightfully exceed normal parameters and expected achievements. But these people are the exception. Any such individual performance variance should trigger a comprehensive review by independent consultants or outside agencies. Unfortunately, the self-serving temptation not to spoil the "goose that lays the golden eggs" on the part of the other leaders often stops such reviews from being done.

There is a postscript to the Admiral Halsey story. Not many people know that Halsey was slated to command our carrier group at the Battle of Midway during the early and critical days of the Pacific War in WWII. Our subsequent victory at sea stopped the Imperial Japanese Navy from invading Hawaii. Had the overly-aggressive Halsey been in command of our fleet at that time, the outcome might have been different. Instead, Halsey had to listen to the Midway battle reports from the confines of a hospital bed, where he was being treated by the U.S. Navy doctors for a severe case of psoriasis!

Notes

Leadership Lessons From History
Part 55

Title: "Strategic Thinking"

All leaders eventually face this situation: a strategic decision needs to be made, and made quickly, but your subordinates/consultants/experts are equally divided on which course to pursue. Worse, yet, the two most widely supported viewpoints recommend completely opposite actions! What should a leader do? Below are a few examples of what others have done in the past.

During WWI, a number of American and British admirals got together to discuss possible solutions to the many allied merchant ships being sunk in the Atlantic Ocean by predatory German submarines. Half the admirals backed a plan to group all the cargo and transport ships into convoys as they sailed across the Atlantic; the other half complained that this was akin to "putting all your eggs into one basket." Any enemy submarine coming upon the convoy could torpedo all the ships! Luckily for the Allies, they ended up choosing the right strategy.

During the American Civil war, an arms manufacturer presented his lever-action, repeating Henry rifle to the North for adoption into the Union Army. Its great rate of fire was a significant improvement over the current long arms, a single-shot breach cartridge or a muzzle-loaded percussion rifle. Nonetheless, the Army decided not to adopt the repeating rifle as it was believed this would lead to their soldiers wasting ammunition. (As it turned out, many Union Soldiers ended up purchasing the repeating rifle and its ammunition with their own money.) Years later, in another example of "army intelligence" saner heads prevailed and the 1903 Springfield rifle, one of the best arms of any war, was converted from the 30-3 round to accept the more powerful 30-06 cartridge. Just recently I read where, starting in the 1980s, the U.S. Army changed — degraded — the rate of twist on the barrels on the M16A2/M4 rifles to accommodate the military's standard tracer round, but in doing so it greatly worsened the weapons' accuracy while simultaneously reducing their effective range.* Which was the right priority for war?

Lastly, in 1900, Major Walter Reed needed funding for his studies on the origin of yellow fever. Unless outbreaks of yellow fever could be controlled, there was no possibility of the Panama Canal ever being dug. However, the U.S. surgeon general was against the project, mostly because his own past experiments (erroneously) had shown that yellow fever WAS NOT spread by mosquitoes. The current military governor of Cuba, after the Spanish-American War, was Leonard Wood, a physician by training who had won the Medal of Honor during the Apache Wars and who had been the original Coronel of the Rough Riders, before turning over command to Theodore Roosevelt. Wood used $10,000 of his police fund to back Walter Reed and his studies. The rest is history: the Panama Canal ended up being one of the most important strategic advantages the United States possessed. Interesting enough, nearly forty years prior, during the Civil War, the Union commander of the occupied city of New Orleans, Major General Benjamin Butler, averted a yellow fever outbreak by ordering the simultaneous carrying out of both plans presented to him by his medical experts, one of which accidentally reduced all the standing water in the metropolis, thereby greatly reducing the mosquito population in the city!

Conclusion

While I don't advocate physicians and other medical personnel misappropriating funding for non-approved projects, the above examples do have a common point: leaders need to always align their strategies to the overall goal or purpose of the organization. Which of several goals has the highest priority? Which priorities are "make or break" points? Are there any precedents? Leaders also need to be flexible, inventive, and adaptable. Foremost, leaders must recognize when expert advice may be self-serving or represent the biases of those who present them. This is especially true in Medicine, where there is a need to remember that all current medical knowledge is limited by its own times.

---

* Plaster J. L. *It Has To Be Green*. American Rifleman. June 2014; pp. 58-63

Notes

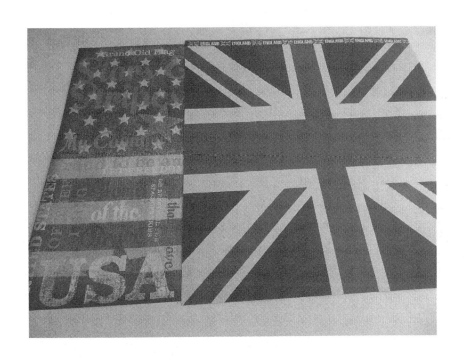

Leadership Lessons From History
Part 56

Title: "True Pay-for-Performance"

A common modern cost-saving business strategy is to either declassify job levels and positions downward, or re-assign job functions to be performed by lower-tiered employees. In doing so, leaders need to be aware of how such actions may disrupt the behind-the-scenes social networks necessary for long-term success, both inside and outside of the organization. It also creates a business environment where successful people are denied the appropriate compensation to go along with their recognition; this is an unhealthy business situation as your most valuable people will have an incentive to work elsewhere. The below story is an example of how even a powerful leader can be stymied by small-minded individuals and their stingy budgets.

Winston Leonard Spencer Churchill (b. 1874- d. 1965) graduated 8th from the Royal Military Academy at Sandhurst (Tactics & Fortifications). He went on to serve as a reporter in the Cuban revolt against Spain. (He loved the cigars!) He then was a correspondent in the Boers War in South Africa. Elected to the House of Commons in 1900 at the age of 26 years, he went on to become the First Lord of the Admiralty in 1911 where he was responsible for converting England's navy ships from coal to oil. During WWI, became the minister of munitions and was instrumental in the development of its nation's first tank forces. After WWI, he served as War Secretary. Subsequently, after losing his seat in the House of Commons, he returned as First Lord of the Admiralty in 1939 and pushed for a stronger AIR FORCE. He became Prime Minister of England twice, 1940 & 1951 and won the 1953 Nobel Prize for Literature. He was knighted in 1953 and made an honorary U.S. citizen in 1963 (his mother was a U.S. citizen).

Right after winning the air "Battle Of Britain," in August 1940, Winston Churchill gave a speech to Parliament and to the English nation, in which he said:

> "Never in the field of human conflict was so
> much owed by so many to so few."

What most do not know is that Churchill was a lifetime supporter of air power. One author* stated: "The admiration for the Royal Air Force (RAF) of Churchill, twice First Lord of the Admiralty, was unconditional." This admiration was especially true by the pilots as Churchill repeatedly lobbied for higher pay and rank for them. You see, while many of the RAF pilots were sergeants, their leaders were officers; U.S. pilots were officers. This difference in rank immediately had an unrecognized social impact in that non-officers could not eat, sleep, or mingle together with officers of any nation, even when they were on leave in London. Their lower pay and rank literally drove a wedge between the regular RAF pilots and their commanders and fellow allied pilots, reducing efficiency and morale. And that brings me to the point of this example.

There is an urban legend regarding a "lost" double context phrase, deleted at the last moment from Churchill's speech about the Battle of Britain, regarding Parliament's parsimonious and unfair treatment of its pilots. Reportedly, Winston's full speech went something like this:

> "Never in the field of human conflict was so
> much owed by so many to so few ..."
>
> "... and for so little!"

---

*   Hough R, Richards D. *The Battle of Britain*. W.W. Norton & Company, 1989:199.

Made in the USA
Middletown, DE
11 May 2016